ISBN 978-0-9972976-0-7

For information on quantity discounts or any other type of requests please email at info@theonlinestorefront.com

Table of Contents

INTRODUCTION

"Find what sparks a light in you, and you will illuminate the world"
DeAnna Kennedy

When the sky would finally begin to darken on the fourth of July, we'd wait impatiently for the fireworks to begin. That's when my father would break out the box of sparklers, those skinny sticks with the gray stuff painted on the ends. I had no idea that it contained a metallic fuel (aluminum, iron or titanium) and an oxidizer such as potassium nitrate or barium nitrate. I only knew breathtaking anticipation, waiting for the touch of flame to turn my world into an exploding, magical place of dancing stars. I would hold the sparkler high and write my name in the blackness, with delirious enjoyment, as a million new sparkles filled the night sky. But oh no! Wait!! The inevitable moment would arrive when it would spit-sputter out, and if I wasn't careful, I'd even burn my fingers – a very unhappy ending to such a delightful experience.

For many people, the desire to get paid for something entrepreneurial similarly flares out all too quickly. After the initial elation, just like a sparkler, they're left feeling disappointed, burned and casting about for the next bright sparkler to come along, the next big idea out there…somewhere!

But let's stop for a moment right here…to ruminate on something that might be extremely intriguing to you: What if the next best idea could come from you? What if instead of depending on someone else to come up with the next firework to illuminate your world for steady compensation, you consider the possibility of creating that 'sparkler' of light yourself, from your very own thoughts? You, yes you are capable of becoming a 'thought generator' filled with inspiration and expertise to share with others. I'm assuring you, it is within you.

Let me be blunt at this point, what I'm talking about is not just the act of "thinking profound thoughts". It's the quality of action you take from your thoughts and the quality of action taken by others inspired by your thoughts that will create the high value and weighty impact for you. I define Thought Leadership as: The art of creating, recognizing and embracing new thoughts, concepts, ideas and inspirations for the purpose of igniting action in oneself and in others.

If you've been instinctual and providential, maybe you've already discovered your natural talents and tendencies and experienced successes and easier times. However, for most of us this just hasn't been the case. If you've denied, or at the very least suppressed, your talent tendencies (resulting in choices other than what you have innate propensity for) you've already discovered the difficulties in finding true reward. My purpose for writing this book is to show you how to reach down deep, grab up what you have natural proclivity for, ignite it, and release it to the world for sale!

As you begin with step one, allow blocks of uninterrupted time. Take time to seriously reflect on activities that you're drawn to or have been drawn to in the past. Take time to think about things you enjoy doing just for the fun or ease doing it. It might be your hobby, or it might be something you feel a sense of satisfaction from doing just because you do it well. Others have probably remarked how well you do this thing. Perhaps you've modestly brushed it off or passed it off as not much of anything because it took so little effort.

Think back to when you were a kid, what caught your attention? What was it that you couldn't turn away from back then? What was it that interested you to the point of wanting to do this or be that someday? Maybe even to this day "that something" is still interesting to you. Let your mind drift along to those daydreams, both past and present.

Time goes by so quickly. Days, months, and years evaporate. We forget what our early aspirations, ambitions and personal wishes were. High school and college rotates our objectives toward practicalities such as career, vocation and paying bills. Most of us lose our "authentic selves" during this time, focusing rather on responsibilities and good jobs. Our authentic core talent objectives are put on the back shelf, and we seldom get around to revisiting those early hopes and desires.

It isn't until we catch ourselves conjecturing what greater success would be affording us on our wish list today, that we regret not having followed up on our dreams back then.

- I sure wish I could be retiring early.

- I really need more retirement funds.

- I so wish I had more time to myself.

- I wish I could quit my job.

- I'd hoped to bring my spouse home from his/her job by this time.

- I long to improve my family's lifestyle.

- I so want to provide college education funds for my kids and grandkids.

- I crave to be able to travel whenever I want to.

- I wish I could contribute more care for our elderly parents.

- I want to be able to give more.

Sound familiar? These kinds of wishes and desires compel us to search opportunities for additional income and force us to look back to a dream we once had. However, as quickly as a spark lights up our impulse for a business deal or opportunity of some sort, apprehension swoops in to zap us back into pragmatic resignation with self-talk sounding something like this:

- What the heck am I thinking?
- I don't know enough about this to make it work!
- Why do I waste my time and money thinking there's something for me?
- Nothing has ever worked for me.
- Why do I think something will work for me now?
- Maybe I'd be in over my head.

The above worries are legitimate concerns. I felt the same way when I opened my first retail shop that involved signing a lease, ordering merchandise and struggling to market my offerings. I bought many how to books, purchased all the marketing programs I could afford, only to fret greatly as the balance of my start-up dollars moved steadily toward zero. I remember the panicky thoughts I had in those early days:

- What if I couldn't make this work?
- Would the daily sales reach the break even point?
- Had I chosen the right location for my business?
- Had I purchased the right inventory?
- Was my shop visible enough from the street?
- Was my overhead sign large enough and bright enough for people to see?

How I fretted over that overhead sign...ok so maybe the $10,000 price tag had a little something to do with that .... but I just couldn't stop worrying about money. The reality that I was a $7,500 per month leaseholder, with $250,000 in wholesale inventory to pay for, had gripped me! What had I done to myself? Then there was insurance, utilities and employees to think about... and... and... I was a wreck with worry, worry, and more worry! I had spent many hours trying to learn from "brick & mortar" books, only to realize that my success would ultimately come down to MY talents, not theirs. It was at this point that I came to the gut wrenching conclusion that I had stepped away from my authentic core talent and into something I was totally unfamiliar with--something that was extremely risky. I had personally guaranteed a long term lease for my retail space, and I was now left with only two options: sink or swim.

I need to stop right here and tell you something very important. Please take note:

In retrospect, I did not know enough about the business of "brick & mortar" retail to have opened a shop. It was with "ice water thrown in my face" shock that the realization hit me: I had chosen a most difficult path, and it was a path with a lot of resistance. You see, I was discovering the hard way that I had wandered way too far away from my Authentic Core Talent. How did I know that? I was not intuitively good at accounting or being a merchant or buying inventory. It took 15 long years to master those talents, and it wasn't an easy journey. Much to the contrary, it was very tough and time consuming.

What should I have done? Where had I missed "the path of least resistance?" Well, the answer became quite obvious—after crushingly difficult years and a lot of hindsight. I should have stayed within my strengths--my creative artistic talent, my authentic core talent. Even though my shop was beautifully displayed and decorated because of my creative talents, it became clearly evident to me that I did not know enough about the business of "brick & mortar" retail to do more than barely survive. I was left with no time at all for my natural creative talents. To survive, I had to spend every minute of every day in a desperate struggle just to keep my head above water.

So, in light of those discouraging revelations....

Allow me to back up a bit, to a much calmer time for me, it was about five years earlier and before I'd opened my first retail shop. Back to the day I became totally aware of my authentic core talent. I knew something astounding was happening to me on that day! It was a sunny summer afternoon, I was just lazing the day away letting myself be thoroughly overtaken by the splendor and charm of the Mighty Mississippi River! Ahhh yes, ...the breeze, the warm sandy beach to sit on, and my feet dangling in the splashing water. Ohhh yes! I knew this was the place for me to be—a place so very conducive to my wandering, meandering imaginations---a place where I could easily let myself be totally overtaken with my creative thoughts. And so it was on a most magical day, engulfed in my own imaginings, that what happened next would be in fact a "before and after" marker for me!

Let me take you with me, back to that day...
...and back to the riverbank and the sunshine, with my feet dangling in the splashing water. I sat there, slowly becoming aware of little "somethings" rolling and tumbling in the gently churning current. These "somethings" that were bumping at my toes as if for attention, so much so that I felt compelled to reach down for a watery rescue scoop. I opened up my hands, I stared down into wet sparkling eyes and gnarly happy faces looking up at me, as though to say they'd reached their destination, I was astonished! The twinkling in their eyes seemed to be eagerly revealing their quiet little spirits, imploring me to trust they were real, tendering up their faith that I would believe. I was more than

captivated, I was fascinated, I reached down for a few more floating and bobbing "Little Spirits" in the sparkling water thinking, "Hmm River Spirits... I have discovered River Spirits"!! And as I gently tucked the little pieces of wood near me on the warm sandy beach to dry, turning them over to closely scrutinize all their little textures and twinkles, I was overwhelmingly struck with awe and inspiration. I knew their story, and their story needed to unfold and be told!

I could barely breathe with excitement as I ran home to pull out my paints and brushes and get to work creating "spirited" little characters that I could clearly see needed to be brought to life on those bits of cottonwood bark. I had filled up my pail with the little guys, and as I ran along staring out over the water, I recognized hundreds of "kinfolk" nodding and bobbling in the watery sparkles. I swear I heard them shouting out to me, "Take us too! Pick me up! Pick me too!!" I laughed back at them, musing they had already come to life, whispering out over the water, "My Little River Spirits, I have found you, and I will come back for all of you, I promise!"

Out of breath, and with my imagination running wild, I painted my first charming character into life, the beginning of The River Spirit collection. By that afternoon, I had named my little guy The Old Man Spirit, and then excitedly painted 50 more to life! Each one had his own personality, a glint of well-hidden inexplicableness in his eyes that natters (speaks) to the ogler (beholder).

My daughter, Lisa, and I wasted not a moment as we imagined a story about the realm these little guys had come from and what their peculiarities meant (even the beginnings of their curious, beguiling adventures). And so it was with proclamation and a "story card" entitled The Legend the Old Man Spirit, that the River Spirit Kingdom officially came into being. We smiled as they seemed to peer up at us, each with a captivating twinkle in his eye, as if to say they'd be sharing even more little river secrets with us very, very soon! Which of course they did! And soon their stories and mysteries drifted into the beginnings of a book, and River Spirits emerged.

It was at this point and with great delight and anticipation that I took the "Old Man Spirit" to my good friend, Vicki Badavinac, who just happened to be a sales representative. She took one look at them and said, "Ladies! Let me take THIS show on the road!" And that's exactly what she did! Vicki presented our River Spirits to shopkeepers near and far and before long I was painting day and night to keep up with the orders that our Miss Vicky was writing. Here's an astounding fact: within only a few weeks, Vicki had sold more than $55,000 in wholesale orders just within her sales area! Now mid-August, I painted around the clock to fulfill and ship orders the retail stores expected before November. Of course, I loved every minute of it! It didn't take long for Vicky, Lisa, and I to put a sales team together for which we enjoyed wild success from our clan of floating enchantment. To this day, I paint and sell my little River Spirits, turning them loose by the thousands all around the world. They've found their way over land and sea, even onto the White House Christmas Tree as the "Minnesota Handmade Craft of the Year". Their story hasn't ended yet! I have my sights set on a Disney movie!

So, with success and excitement under my belt, along with Vicky's guidance, Lisa and I went on to build a very successful wholesale business with other products that we manufactured. I carefully listened to the creative inspirations flowing to me, heeding and acting on them faithfully. As a result, we designed an interesting line of products that were represented at Merchandise Marts throughout the United States. Looking back on those experiences, I could not imagine assigning an actual dollar value to the education earned by working closely with sales reps, wholesale owners, distributors and retail shop owners! My journey through the manufacturing and distribution process presented me with lessons and relationships of a lifetime. As a matter of fact, many of those early relationships remain with me to this day and have blossomed into treasured lifelong friendships.

So, now from the 'sublime to the arduous'. Let's walk back to my gut wrenching retail days of a few paragraphs ago, back to the days that followed the manufacturing and wholesale successes of the River Spirits, to the days that had unfortunately turned gripping, frantic and scary. I had brought this on myself resulting from my decision to open a 3,000 square foot expensive space, without enough retail knowledge.

I had honestly believed retail was the natural advancement for my business. Unfortunately, I hadn't anticipated the enormous amount of money and time would be quite so dizzying. The overhead was like a voracious animal, hungrily chomping up every nickel and every minute I poured into it, impatiently waiting for its next feeding. It was more than I had ever dealt with, and it took every last penny I had. I was out on the rolling sea in a raft, and it would only take a bit of a wind storm to toss me even farther out into uncharted waters. This is not a place I'd wish for anyone to be.

I'd sincerely thought I knew enough! I kept telling myself to just work harder, "no pain--no gain," right? ... Yep, I foolishly thought a retail shop would be an easy transition, not to mention a real accomplishment! After all, I had just carved out a very special and lucrative niche for myself, and had successfully brought it to the wholesale marketplace. My rationale being that retail should follow as the natural course for even greater success and would be an absolute breeze!

Unfortunately, the breeze I'd anticipated being so delightful and fun…turned into a gigantic, uncontrollable hurricane before I knew it ….and I was blown out into very troubled waters. I was in over my head, and I was about to go down. I had severely miscalculated and was now harshly discovering how much I did not know. How on earth was I going to make it through this?

It's worth re-stating here that without enough education in the business of retail, I had definitely forsaken my authentic core talent in this endeavor, and as a result the path was bumpy, difficult, and it was absolutely not coming easily to me. I was undeniably not on "the path of least resistance."

As if I needed an additional negative revelation, yet another upheaval was dawning on me as big changes befell the world of small business.

Generations of family owned storefronts, (the backbone of most cities, villages, and towns across America) once lovingly passed down with pride, were now being shoved aside for the Big Box stores and the convenience of online retail shopping. I had chosen one of the most difficult times in history to open a "brick & mortar" business.

It was at this point, that I decided to adjust my mind set, take stock of my talents and seriously take action to climb the Mt Everest before me. I made the decision to focus on what I knew best and that was to get back to my "creative self". I knew my creativity could be relied on (and if I could figure out how to make the most of this strength under these circumstances) maybe, just maybe I would be able to navigate my way out of this tempest I had placed myself in.

My first "creative" implementation was a branded coffee bar, making my shop appealing to men and not just women. It almost doubled my traffic flow. People stood in line by 6am ready to buy tasty coffee, lattes, and cappuccinos. Then I added Dippin' Dots and an ice cream bar, hosting birthday parties and other fun events for even more community activity.

My second "creative" step was to bring in Godiva chocolates with all of its elegance and perceived value. I pre-sold fabulous holiday gift baskets (of my design) to major corporations in the Twin Cities area. Sometimes referred to as "unearthing an invisible market", this opened up an entirely new sales opportunity for my floundering retail business.

My third "creative" step was to use my musical talents, gathering musicians around. Soon I had bands playing in my shop every Saturday morning. The shop quickly became a most fun place in my community for friends to socialize and have fun while enjoying coffee and treats.

My final "creative" step was to make the most of my River Spirits, telling their story as a part of the advertising and marketing for the shop. After all, it was up to me to write copy for the newspaper publications and direct marketing opportunities. I told their story as often as I could. I ramped up these stories with offerings of "shopper-tainment" fun in my shop and invited my community to enjoy.

Motivated by the fear of failure, I learned these lessons at break-neck speed—it became standard procedure to just stay afloat. Online shopping was coming into its own with the screaming mantra "Goods and services accessible instantly and delivered at lightning speed!" Convenience and speed now reigned supreme! I clearly remember thinking it mandatory for "brick & mortar" shops to adjust and push forward regarding websites.

Businesses, online and offline at that time were desperately vying for visibility and traffic flow in the changing world of commerce. Local businesses questioned whether or not they needed a website. Emerging online businesses struggled for a firm foothold. It seems silly now, but both online and offline businesses were colonizing new ground. Undoubtedly, early pioneers felt the same as they pulled their wagons into new towns and settlements, amidst wide open territories, to set up shop. What do you suppose the wild west settlers thought as they rolled into the new frontier?

Did they look around town wondering how they could fit in to make a living?
Did they wonder if they had settled in the right town?
Was it scary for them as they tried to figure out what expertise they had within themselves that could be leveraged into a retail or service shop?
Did they worry about having enough money to start their businesses?
How would they get the word out to neighbors and nearby townspeople?

I think our pioneer ancestors were literally looking for the same thing businesses look for today…a way to make money in ever changing, unfamiliar territory.

As the months and years ticked by, I was able to overcome many adversities by relying on my authentic core talent and my retail business began to flourish. If I hadn't taken this course of action, I would not have financially survived. I had made dire mistakes by straying so far from my authentic core talent, I'd thought I would automatically know how to succeed in retail, and I'd struggled mightily as a result.

This is where my story gets significant for you. Today, you have the opportunity to sell anything online without all of the encumbrances of a "brick & mortar" storefront. You have the immediate advantage of reaching millions of people around the world with something as modest as a relevant website. You can become more effective than a traditional, very expensive "brick & mortar" venue.

It's important to note that, although commerce has changed to it's very core, buyers have not changed at all, they still buy goods and services day after day in astounding and ever increasing numbers. They always have and always will! This fact offers the great opportunity for YOU to place your products or service in front of online buyers.

The purpose of How to Find the Talent Within You...and Sell It! is to help you discover the great gift within yourself... just waiting to be unleashed and released for online sales success.

I have developed a proven sequence of steps that will make it easy for you to find your way, in a natural manner, with less effort. You will simply learn to use your core talents, aptitudes, and capabilities. Similar to riding a bicycle, you'll learn by direct personal discovery, and the moment will occur when the ability becomes yours. These steps will help you take advantage of your authentic core talent, and to find your expertise for an effective online and/or offline business. Are you ready? Let's get started!

Ask yourself these 3 questions:
1. "Do I want to jump into the driver's seat and fast forward myself to triumph?"
2. "Am I ready to get moving and take action?"
3. "Am I ready to claim myself an expert and get paid for my thoughts, talents, and expertise?"

Now let me ask you 2 more questions:

1. Are you ready to strike the match to your own sparkler, one that won't flicker and fade?
2. Are you ready to declare your name to the wide expanse of the Internet?

If your answers to most of the questions are YES, keep reading. The following chapters will unveil my ten proven steps to reveal and release the "thought generator" and "thought leader" within you. Imagine originating and ripening your own thoughts, coining and establishing them as your very own, then pushing them out and beyond to even selling them. I call this process a "personal paradigm switch" -- the development of finding your authentic core talent, recognizing your expertise, and viewing yourself in a different light to see something in yourself that you've not identified or taken seriously before. You may be thinking, "I don't think I can see that in myself", but with a little help and direction …you WILL see this in yourself.

So, what do you say we get to work and uncover your talent, embrace its existence and unleash it for the entire world to see? Yield to the expert already within you! Become a "thought generator" and then onto a "thought leader" in your area of expertise. Position yourself to communicate your very own insights and inspirations to the world. Let's get going and reach for the sparkling stars!

STEP 1

WHAT WERE YOU BORN TO DO?

"Self-exploration is the magic ingredient that ignites and fuels your authentic core talent"
DeAnna Kennedy

Creating a future of your own design will begin by questioning and redefining the very nature of what is possible within the authentic you.

The 1st question to ask of yourself is this:
Do I *want* to dig deep to uncover and pursue *the most authentic and successful me*?

It's essential that you commit to self-reflection and observation in this process. You'll be reflecting on experiences when you felt really capable, gifted, clever, competent and proficient. What were you doing when you last *felt effective and sensed talent within yourself?*

You must prepare yourself to take a thoughtful journey! A journey that will evoke your authentic self from beneath the noise and clutter of your everyday life.

The 2nd question to ask of yourself is this:
Do I yearn for a profound and lasting difference in my life?

The process of intense self-discovery typically happens slowly and over time, but within these pages I will present to you the ten steps to finding your *authentic core talent* straightaway. You'll have an action plan to ignite your talent quickly. This ignition triggers your subconscious "special-forces" to hunt down and enable your core talent identity, shifting the very nature of what is possible for you. You'll experience flashes of revelation leading you to proclaim, "YES, this is what I'm good at!" The discoveries, this paradigm shift, will pilot you toward the life you desire, even if it seems to fly you out of your comfort zone momentarily in the process.

Many people feel a bit awkward with change at first, primarily because life keeps us on automatic pilot, so to speak, and very much controlled by what is expected of us within our culture and family. The result, unfortunately, becomes how we define ourselves. Even worse, this definition of ourselves handcuffs the talents we were born with that could have presented *the path of least resistance* and *the most direct route* for our "life map" to success.

Resetting your "life map", with your *authentic core talent* in place *will become automatic* as you implement and exercise your new strengths. Your myelin insulation will steadily increase, wrapping your neural circuits and growing according to certain brain signals. The story of myelin insulation according to Daniel Coyle in his book The Talent Code, is similar to another progression-fostered mechanism you exercise every day: your muscles. It is what physically happens within your brain as you learn any skill. I believe this happens quickly and significantly as you become aware of your *authentic core talent*.
What has long stirred within you?
What flickering of insight do you feel right now?
What have you long yearned to undertake but haven't made allowance for?

Driving your "life vehicle", with one foot on the gas while the other is on the brake, will not sustain forward momentum. You'll have difficulty steering through curves and getting up hills, you'll certainly struggle to stay on course. You'll have little control when it comes to staying on track for the kind of impetus you want. You might be nodding at this point, thinking, "Yep! That sounds like me!"

The 3rd question is actually a series of questions for you to ask of yourself:
How depressed am I with my life or how much of my life is depressing me?
How long have I felt this bored with my life, this lost, and or this left behind?
How far away am I from really feeling alive, enthusiastic, and thankful for what I am doing?

When was the last time I woke up feeling excited and happy about the day ahead?

Whew! After those questions, are you dismayed at how far off course you might be feeling? Ok, when was the last time you felt fully alert and gratified for the sunshine on your skin and the smell of the earth beneath your feet? If you're anything like me, you'll probably come to the same awful conclusion I came to… that the last time I'd really felt that alive was when I was a kid! Ouch! We all had endless imaginations back then didn't we? Barbie dolls gave us endless hours of playing house and Superman capes gave us special flying powers, the imaginings of childhood. Do you remember declaring, "I want to be an astronaut or a piano player or a ballerina" or something of the like? We had great expectations for ourselves didn't we? We hadn't yet heard the "you'd better" and "you should" forewarnings.

At this point, I'd like to share some happenings from my life, to give you a few examples to consider of how authentic core talent can show up early in life and really never leave.
My first entrepreneurial endeavor began with my love for music. I'd been singing from childhood with my family, in church and high school events. I found real and complete joy in the process of making music. It didn't take long to figure out that if I wanted to be in the music business, I had better figure out how to create opportunities to make money at it. So, with early lessons from my grandfather, uncles and aunts, I gathered together my own tribe of musicians and began traveling around the country. We did what musicians love doing the most – we played music! My family played various instruments and we all sang. I was continually inspired to get better at my talent. I tried my hand at writing songs and recording in Nashville, I even had my own local television show for a few years. It was an exhilarating time for me, and it all came so very easily!

I realized (by watching the big guys in the industry) that there was more to this than just playing music and singing, and that if I wanted to make a real business out of what I loved doing, I had better get busy. I found increased confidence by lifting the bar higher and higher for myself, such as adding "booking agent" to my list of accomplishments. I taught myself how to buy name acts from national entertainment agencies, and resell them as packaged deals to state & county fairs and business conventions (These were early retail lessons for sure, but I didn't realize it at the time!). I performed as the 'opening act' for these shows, providing excellent venues and much larger paychecks for my band and myself. It was great fun working with artists such as George Strait, Eddy Raven, Crystal Gayle, Merle Haggard, Sylvia, Jana Jae, Rex Allen Jr, The Nitti Gritty Dirt Band, and many more. I was experiencing the time of my life and living my passion, this was certainly a dream come true for me.

Soon, I was making enough money to build a professional recording studio. I hired a studio engineer, and my "tribe" and I wrote and recorded jingles for numerous national companies including Stihl Chainsaw, Ace Hardware, The United States Marines, and well as many smaller businesses. I'd sharpened my sales ability during this time and found I really enjoyed bringing quality product to the marketplace. This was such an amazing experience and the new opportunities just kept opening up in front of me.

My daughter, Lisa, was born during this time, and I took her everywhere with me. She would happily sit in the front row or back stage, prompting lyrics to me (being the fast little study she's always been!) I vividly recall thinking back then, how incredibly lucky I was to be working at something I thoroughly enjoyed and have my baby girl right there with me. I knew that many parents anguished over difficult choices, balancing their work hours with family responsibilities, I felt hugely fortunate to have it all!

Around this time, "dot-coms" were entering mainstream and it became crystal clear that I would need to learn everything I could and stretch yet again…to keep pushing forward. Notice, if you will, that I had used my authentic core talent of creativity to propel myself as far forward. This happened well before I was conscious of why it was working for me. The doors kept opening, providing me with "the path of least resistance" because I was using my natural gift.

My second entrepreneurial love became art, obviously another creative. However, I didn't discover that artistic ability in myself until I moved away from my hometown in Wisconsin. Why? Because I didn't have the confidence. My mother and my brother are both fine artists, it was one thing for me to enjoy painting but quite another experience to do so amidst their talent. Observing them, I was so in awe of their talent, I dared not pick up a paint brush anywhere near them. However, (when I moved away from my family) I was able to push through that boundary, and claim a second passion. This second passion would be to create and sell my artwork. I absolutely loved creating works of art and selling them!

I'd moved to St Paul, and the Mississippi River greatly influenced my creativity. It inspired me to let my artistic bent flow and flourish, much like the river. To this day, I can't get enough of the gnarled roots on the river banks, the sparkling rocks and rushing current of this magnificent river, it's daily music to my eyes and ears. I discovered that those living along the mighty river were filled with inspiration and a deep sensitivity for nature....and so it happened to me as well.

This is where The River Spirit adventure began. This is where my imagination and artistic talent led me to find my niche in the art world. This journey with my "Old Man Spirit" and his family of River Spirits is not yet complete. There's another book, and hopefully a movie deal ahead. I'm still pursuing that dream!

My brand new infatuation is now my third entrepreneurial love, I can barely put the camera down these days. The objects for my documentation seem to present their beauty everywhere I look, and I can't stop looking! The challenge to get THE shot always excites me and keeps me searching for the next find of even the smallest of little gems out there, just waiting to be discovered. I thrive on finding perfect shots and turning them into works of art to sell. "River Gem Photography" began with pursuing that passion and my cell phone camera. I was realizing the GREAT power in discovering yet another facet of my authentic core talent!

As my creative and entrepreneurial spirit evolved, I clearly recognized why my successes had come along effortlessly. It was also clear to me why the harsh, tough times I'd experienced had stopped me in my tracks. I realized that I had tapped into something quite profound – something that consistently presented me with "the path of least resistance" as long as I stayed true to my authentic core talent.

Today, I come alongside others, aligning my authentic core talent to help trigger successes.
Developmental psychologist, Erik Erickson, calls what I do "generativity" – the desire to teach others from one's experiences.

Acting on a "given gift" is an incredibly scary thing for many. It brings out feelings of vulnerability and possibly fills us full of pre-emptive self-doubt. As children, we are trained out of and away from our gifts because of the collective fear of that which is uncertain. We're encouraged not to trust our impulses, imagination, intuition, instincts, and loves. Instead we're taught to follow rules and embrace pragmatic values.

Now, don't get me wrong here, paying the bills is important, and I'm not saying that you should renounce accountability in favor of foolishly running off in an unknown direction. However, recognizing the importance of your natural imaginations, intuitions, instincts and early loves (and using your talents with real intention) are essential for the successes in your life.
Have you daydreamed of becoming a painter, a writer, a public speaker, a philosopher, a photographer, a fishing guide, a lodge owner, a leader of some kind? If you've had thoughts of seizing more for your life, you have definitely provoked and activated something deep within yourself. It is the reason you're in front of this information today.

And here's even better news. You're here at the best time in history **for real income using your very own thoughts and ideas.** You might be wondering if you have the kind of talent to create your own success. Here's a tip to calm your nerves: you may not have all you need to achieve today, but you DO have knowledge enough to get started today, and with a helping hand to uncover your *authentic core talent* (even if you *swear* you don't have a core talent or expertise) I'm declaring to you RIGHT NOW that YOU DO. Without delay you can become a "thought generator" a "thought leader" and the master of your destiny!

I've witnessed people with dashed hopes, standing on the banks of the Mississippi River, skipping stones far out onto the water, watching them bounce one, two, three times and sink into silence. Much like their optimism and aspiration, their dwindled dreams have left them with what *might* have been *if only*, ... *if only*! On the other hand, I've watched others take on the task of conquering the width and current of the mighty river by *finding* the most manageable point, 'the path of least resistance' to skip their pebbles confidently across to the other side. They know they could ultimately walk across the mighty river (at a manageable point) albeit stepping out onto slippery, sometimes wet stones to feel the power of accomplishing things seemingly unachievable to others.

Steps like the above, while seemingly risky... are yours to take.

Get up from the shore of YOUR mighty river...

Find your path of least resistance...

Put YOUR feet solidly on a few headwater stones...

Go forward to where you want to see yourself being...

Say to the spirit of life within you *I CAN DO THIS!!* ...*and STEP FORWARD!*

STEP 2

GET YOUR ACT TOGETHER!
YOUR UNIQUE IDENTITY

"Ask yourself what it is that makes you come alive...then go out and do that thing!
DeAnna Kennedy

Nearly every day I hear people say, "I hate my job, I hate my cubicle and I hate my life! Is there a way to change this boring, repetitive life? What can I do to make a significant change in my life?"

My response? I've been in and around business my entire life, and I can tell you with great certainty that we are living in *the* most unique times ever!

Change #1: The Internet has profoundly leveled the commerce playing field, once only open to companies with enormous budgets and buildings, it's now open to people like you and me with home or garage offices!

Change #2: Traditional commerce has morphed into wildly successful e-commerce.

These two changes alone...have opened up opportunities for any and all who want to throw their hat into the commerce/e-commerce ring for significant impact on the general buying public.
The ease with which YOU can now set up shop from your home office, garage or even a shed in the backyard is astounding. It no longer matters WHERE a business is located.

Most of us do not know how to apply these fabulous opportunities of change to ourselves. Once you have figured out what your 'Authentic Core Talent' is...you are in the perfect position to embrace your talent, tell your story and sell something.
I'd like you to pay special attention right here:

It begins with **YOU** and uncovering your *authentic core talent* or your *ACT* and the ***inspirations*** that always follow!

So, what do you say we move forward and Get Your Act Together?

Let's explore a bit with the little exercise below:
If money were not an obstacle, and all the roadblocks were miraculously removed, in what activity would you choose to participate in? (This eliminates the option of sitting on the couch all day eating popcorn and watching reality television, unless of course your gift is spotting hit television shows and taste-testing popcorn.)

Keep your eyes closed and let your mind drift along, maybe drifting back to where it use to go as a child or back to your high school days when everything was an exciting adventure before you.
What did you love?
What did you think you would be when you grew up?

Keep thinking; let these thoughts bubble on up to the surface. Ask yourself:

"What do I like? And what do I enjoy doing that I know a lot about?"
"What comes naturally to me, maybe even so naturally I tend to take it for granted?

The talents that come most naturally to us are the talents we are most likely to overlook, to *not* seriously acknowledge *because* they come so easily to us. Think about that for a minute! We've pretty much been conditioned to think that we must endure great pain and struggle to achieve something worthwhile. No pain, no gain, right? I would rather make the most of what I'm naturally good at, not to mention have significant talent for, than struggle -- wouldn't you?

It turns out that *our passions and interests are quite visible at a very young age*, much younger than first thought. Scientist have discovered that our core personality traits *stay very much intact throughout adulthood*, we just get very proficient at suppressing them.

Here's an example: When I was six or seven years old, my uncle took to me see a couple of Disney movies, *Snow White* and *Cinderella*. I was profoundly struck by the character animation. The movie became so very real to me that I literally got lost in it, my imagination totally taking me over. During that time frame of my young life, the very same uncle taught musical rhythm to me, how to snap my fingers and tap my toes to keep time. Oh, what fun! He followed up by teaching me how to sing harmony to his melody. It was exhilarating to me! I want you to know that experiences similar to mine have in all probability happened to you too... a little nudge here, a little whisper there. Think back on experiences in your life that stand out above the rest in your memories. They're still there within you.... waiting to surface and be acknowledged! Both early experiences still resonate powerfully within me to this very day.

I have never drifted very far away from those treasured experiences shared with my uncle! I truly believe that he tapped into my *authentic core talent*, my *ACT*, at that early age. He obviously had similar gifts and talents, and by sharing them with me, he unwittingly helped me *get my ACT together!* Those early sparks of inspiration would stay ignited within me for a lifetime of successes. Has there been someone in your life like my uncle?

Try this little experiment for the next few days: Pay attention to the little whispers that pass through your mind as you go about your daily activities and relaxations. They'll come along in the form of unexpected thoughts that flutter through your consciousness, usually with unexpected enthusiasm and energy attached. You might hear yourself say (or think) any of the following phrases:

- Well, THAT was fun!
- Wow!! THAT was easier to do than I thought it would be!
- I'd LOVE to do THAT again!
- I wish I had a week to just do THIS!!
- I HAVE to do THIS again!!
- Hey, I'm GOOD at THIS!

Now, find a notebook and write down what you were doing when you felt this kind of energy and enthusiasm! Don't forget to note your actual verbal self-confirmation phrase or phrases.

After you've paid attention to a few unexpected bursts of exhilaration, take some time to find quietness and reflect on them, then seriously have a conversation with yourself and ask:

- What am I easily inspired to do?
- Do I find myself drawn to certain things/activities over and over?
- Are there things I love to do, just for the sake of doing?

Now, back to your notebook to make lists of your personal attention grabbers:

- Your talent or talents
- The activities you love
- Activities and work that come easily to you but maybe difficult for others
- The things you are easily inspired to do

By recognizing and observing your *Authentic Core Talent*, you are literally *Getting Your ACT Together!* You are tapping into your *core identity* and unveiling your *personal path of least resistance.*

- Document your observations
- Document your enthusiasm levels.
- Document your reactions

As you continue to make observations, you'll find your head filling up with inspirations. Where are these inspirations taking you in thought? Note the ideas beginning to flow within you. How many things long forgotten are you remembering, like the first time you picked up a fishing rod or saw someone making their own fishing lures? Maybe your earlier memories will be of canoeing or planting flower seeds or pumpkin seeds in your grandma's garden. Perhaps it was loving the hunt to find antique fabric and being able to fashion beautiful handbags from your find.

A few years ago while in New York City, I wandered into a stunning little shop, a great example of what I'm talking about. I was in awe as the shop owner, Lorraine Kirke, shared her delightful story of Geminola with me. She spoke of traveling the world over in search of fabulous fabrics, used and new, and the wonderful adventures she'd had in doing so. Upon returning home, she expertly fashioned her finds into beautiful dresses, bags and accessories. All of her creations were one of a kind designs and extremely sought after by stars such as Sex and the City's Sarah Jessica Parker. Lorraine has created an extraordinary business from her love of beautiful fabrics, her incredible design talent, and her wanderlust sense of adventure. She has a story to tell and fabulous fashions to sell! www.geminola.com

A concept such as Lorraine's awaits somewhere within all of us… waiting to unfold and be told. Dig down and discover what it is that sparks your heartfelt inspirations and turn those inspirations into your great identity, and *get your ACT together!*

As you practice this kind of thinking, an almost magical paradigm switch will appear before your very own eyes. This "Great Identity" quest can alter your assumption that working for a living has to be endured, into the delightful revelation that working at what you love doing is THE most exciting adventure EVER!!

Author Thomas Kuhn used the duck-rabbit optical illusion to demonstrate the way in which a paradigm shift could cause us to see information in an entirely different way. I love this example, because it demonstrates the focus it takes to see something different for yourself while living the life you're used to living! The transition is yours, focus on yourself *with* your talent, and you'll see yourself from a different view, and with much more enthusiasm!

Are you intrigued by this path of thinking? Because it comes with an attached bonus of energy that you cannot deny!

This is the "thinking path" I've been walking since childhood, always challenging myself to view the very ordinary in search of spotting something quite extraordinary, undiscovered by most others! My "thinking path" has exposed boundless opportunities, from recognizing a million-dollar product idea on the riverbank of the Mississippi River, to standing beside George Strait and others, on event stages. I've built a recording studio and written jingles for the US Marines, manufactured products, sold wholesale and then retail in my search of mastering the art of the sale. Recently, I brought in $60,000 in just one hour, walking 12 clients through a building, looking at cool products and introducing them to my long-time business friends. Getting my *ACT* together, discovering my *authentic core talent*, and listening to the inspirations that followed have served me very well! You'd better believe I intend to continue paying attention to these inspirations of pure gold!

My recommendation to you is to pay attention to yourself and become more alert to your own thoughts! It's critically important for you to discover your *ACT* so that your inspirations materialize! Your very own inspirations will lead you to finding your great identity .... and the creation of a brand-able business if you so choose.

Below, consider a few magical sparks that are likely to make an appearance as you discover your authentic core talent and expose great identity within you:

- Your Great Identity will take on a life of its own
- Your Great Identity will provide a solid foundation for recognition, your platform
- Your Great Identity easily attracts others
- Your Great Identity will be easy to remember, difficult to forget
- Your Great Identity will lift a great deal of weight all by itself
- Your Great Identity will speak loudly for itself without explanation
- Your Great Identity can become your brand, if you choose
- Your Great Identity will write your name in the sky for all to see

Ok, so now it's time for a few brainstorming questions for you to consider:

- Where might be your *Authentic Core Talent* be leading you?
- Are you beginning to experience sparks of inspiration?
- Are you inspired to act on them instead of letting them remain tucked away somewhere?
- What specific activities are you drawn to and could see yourself being a part of?

The following are four clues indicating you are discerning your authentic core talent and are on the right path to discovering your own great identity:

Clue #1 - As you are finding your *Authentic Core Talent*, you will feel as if you've re-united with an old friend. You'll find yourself thinking thoughts that are in alignment with you as a person and they feel achievable. It becomes obvious to you that struggling to be something in conflict with or apart from your *Authentic Core Talent* feels the more difficult trail to travel and of little interest to you.

Ask yourself this question: What can I offer to myself, as well as others utilizing my *Authentic Core Talent?*

Clue #2 - Your identity becomes the solid foundation for your platform of information. It paves a direct and clear path with clear and apparent information, revealing what you and your talent are about.

Example: www.atouchofhaiti.com Please meet Fran, from New York City. She's a corporate executive during the day. However, more and more, Fran felt the pull to do something more nourishing to her soul and helpful for the people of Haiti, home in her heart! Fran offers hand-crafted art, jewelry, and music from her online storefront. Much of it is made in Haiti by local craftsmen/women. She found the "it" she'd been searching for...and now she has IT in spades!! Fran is loving her very successful online storefront.

Clue #3 - The image identifying your talent is easily apparent. Have you heard stories of CB radio operators back in the day? 10-4 Good Buddy? Primarily used by over the road truck drivers, CB'rs cleverly chose a "handle" to quickly identify and differentiate themselves from other truckers out there on the highway. Today, in the noisy world of the internet, the same principle is applicable. Your great identity is your unique handle, shouting out to information seekers, "Hey, here I am! Look at me. Listen to me. I'm different from everyone else! I have what you're looking for!" It quickly grabs attention and traction, convincing information seekers that they are in the right place!

Example: www.thenestingchick.com   What image comes to mind when you read "The Nesting Chick"? Please meet Ruth, a Jersey chick. Her unique identity indicates a focus on nesting... hmm that's interesting, AND it provokes curiosity. Is she an empty nester? Is she feathering a new nest? Does she sell nesting furniture, vessels or dishware? Maybe all of the above...we certainly know from her .com that she's an interesting chick!   Ruth is loving how she can now bring her special talent to the world.

Clue #4 - Your identity shouts out loudly for itself without explanation, perhaps even speaking to the solutions being offered. This *great identity* will help seekers feel they have found solutions for their dilemma in you, and stay with you longer. Whether it's the perfect indoor outdoor rug, a load of topsoil delivered for the garden, a flamingo themed piece of art, or the perfect organizational shelf for an RV or houseboat, your name should shout out your identity.

Example: Please meet Karen, from Ottawa, Canada, Karen's family has been in the RV business for 53 years. Karen had searched for years to find an interesting way to sell product online, but nothing seemed to keep her interest. Then, she and I connected and dug into her authentic core talents. We discovered that Karen is a super organizer, that she loves every aspect of the relationship between space and energy. What did Karen know the most about? Well, RV's of course. She now offers organizational products for campers, RVers, and basic small spaces. This concept was there for her all along. She just hadn't recognized it, because she was too close to her family business. She had overlooked where she had the most experience and talent! Now she has become the real expert at bringing organization to many varieties of small spaces!

Here's another prodigious example: www.sandyscherff.com   If you're a Baby Boomer, the biggest challenge may come with reimagining yourself and your career. Please meet Sandy Scherff, a Boomer herself, she speaks to these needs through her website. She knows this demographic is adapting to a new environment as they plan to alternate between periods of work and leisure. Although they represent only 32 percent of the U.S. population, Americans over 50 control 77 percent of the total net worth and have nearly $46 trillion of wealth, according to the Bureau of Labor Statistics. Sandy offers exciting ideas for Boomers living a vigorous life. By 2030, more than one in three Americans will be over 50. These 50-year-olds are nothing like the generations that came before them. They want to try new things, travel and explore. Rather than tired, this generation is entering a new stage of life with energy, drive and high expectations. For them, retirement is the start of new adventures.

Sandy says "Baby boomers are looking for ways to stay challenged and vital, they do not want to be considered old. Their focus has moved from *things*, to *experiences* like travel and recreation." She says, "Boomers are living longer and wanting to maintain their health, they want to make the second half of their lives really count." Sandy knows that learning is a lifelong undertaking, and that aging learners have the freedom to study what they love, learning new things, starting new businesses and staying actively engaged. She says safety and comfort are also highly regarded considerations, every day new and less complicated technology is introduced. Check out Sandy's website, she's tuned in to satisfying the needs of baby boomers and keeping them updated as the demographic shift expands in the coming decade.

Then there's Rebecca Aspan (the self-proclaimed Lingerie Evangelist) a good example of how she has followed her inspiration and expertise. She began with her Greenwich Village storefront, La Petite Coquette (translated as The Little Flirt). What a great identity! As a lingerie enthusiast, she has the desire to "spread the good word and supply the women of Greenwich Village with sexy, chic undergarments that fit well". She tells her story in the book, *Lessons in Lingerie*. She opened her tiny shop at the site of a former kosher rotisserie chicken outlet, and as she phrases it, "trade one kind of breast for another". Now her website copy continues her story, as she involves herself in "educating, empowering, and uplifting those who enter her temple of pink and satin, encouraging, and celebrating 'the little flirt' in every woman". The talent discovery, the identity, the story, the window-dressing, the copy – all flowing together to make Rebecca Aspan the go-to "Bra Sage" in Greenwich Village and yes, virtually all around the world.

To sum up: The pure enjoyment of doing something you love doing, fueled by your *authentic core talent*, is the perfect recipe for wild success. Embrace your *authentic talent*, pay attention to the inspirations as they fire their way into your consciousness. Make sure your aspirations stay true to your *authentic core talent*. Keep your sites fixed on your authentic talent first. Here's a hint: Think of your *authentic core talent* as a pair of binoculars to view your life through. This will help you re-define your identity and your story. You'll find if you follow this track you'll be running wildly down your very own *path of least resistance* and onto your ultimate and successful destination in life!

Here's a tip: Keep in mind that an over inflated sense of self won't empower you; it will actually hold your "authentic self" hostage, inhibiting and stopping the flow of energy through you. Make sure your identity speaks to the people you are connecting with and doesn't just speak of you. Focus on activities that will engage and connect you with others to become a facilitator of your talent. See yourself inspiring countless people with your work to enrich *their* lives with your words, thoughts, deeds, and products. Feel yourself being the breezeway through which energy flows from you to others, with clear benefits for those before you. It will effortlessly flow back to you!

STEP 3

TELL YOUR STORY

"You are the most magnificent thing you possess
The sound of your voice, your thoughts, your identity, your story
So write with your heart, draw from your beauty, create from your
soul, play, dance and live as only you can"
DeAnna Kennedy

Once you've gotten your *ACT* together, and your *great identity* is screamin' obvious, it'll be time to tell your very own story. This will become a part of your platform of information...your story, exclusively and distinctively your own... the beating heart of who you are.

No one can tell YOUR story like you can! It's a story that applies to you and ONLY YOU! It becomes a magnetic force that will attract others to YOU. Your story will pull audiences in, presenting a true and vulnerable look at who you are, and giving others an inimitable view of you.

The more compelling and emotionally charged your story is, the more irresistibly interesting you will become. Keep in mind that most attachments or bonds occur when emotional connection strikes. A good story can become just such a hook for you, drawing people in and keeping them rapt.

Identity, product, or service successes will always come down to the number of eyes enticed. A compelling story will trump almost every other piece of the marketing puzzle. It's THAT important!

Take, for example, the designer/owner who creates exquisite keepsakes and high end table favors for celebrity weddings and other grand celebratory events. This owner's inspirational story goes all the way back to 6th grade when she hand painted keepsake place cards for Thanksgiving and Christmas tables at the local women's shelter in her community. She spent countless hours getting to know every single guest throughout the year, gathering their favorite colors and interests like festive bouquets. She would then design beautiful place cards using their collective favorite watercolor hues, hand lettering each name with detailed attention, and adding her heartwarming original poetry. She was loved by all. Later, in high school as homecoming queen, she meticulously fashioned hundreds of beautiful flowers from colorful tissues, eliciting help from dozens of "her" kids from the children's hospital cancer wing, where she lovingly volunteered her time. Each flower was tied with an elegant nametag, hand lettered with the name of the child whose little fingers had helped create the fluffy petals. With flowing satin ribbons, she attached each child's flower to her father's red corvette convertible. "Her kids" would now be a part of the homecoming parade.

You can easily see how her creative beginnings would have carved the path toward distinctive table favors she now elegantly designs and fashions for events of Hollywood personalities. She has even caught the attention of White House planners over the years. She now creates keepsakes around the world for prestigious events and ceremonies, her early story serving as poignant testimony to her exquisite detailed designs for brides and event planners. She ensures their event will be grand and unforgettable! Compare her story to someone not having a memorable story and inescapable credibility!

Consider someone who has sold fishing bait and tackle. The owner's stories spoke to grandpa's secret fishin' hole in the north woods, still growing monster muskies and accessible only by native guides. A favorite story describes the necessity to bend a muskie fish like a banana in order to get it into the bed of his pickup truck, fish tail and fish head pointing skyward. He also tells of another incredible catch landed by his own son, a ten-year-old kid using his own hand tied fishing lure made from discarded bird feathers, bits of old wire and his mom's broken earring. Who was the family that owned that shop? Oh yes! It was the Texaco gas & bait shop called "The Minnow Bucket" in Lac du Flambeau, Wisconsin, a location thousands of tourists flocked to during the summer months. Hmmm, how do I know all of these details? Well, that's part of my story too!

Are you seeing what the common thread for the teacher, the keepsake artist and the organizer is? Of course, each one has a compelling story! The take away for you is this...we really all have a story! That thought bears repeating ...*each* of us really do have a story! Think of your story as an interesting book cover, it's colorful, enticing, beckoning one and all to read within to find out more.

An author might invite his reader to peek into his anguished struggle with writer's block during the writing trek of his very first novel. He might re-count how the breakthrough inspiration came to him after finding a single scrap of paper wedged beneath a board in a dilapidated shack, his childhood fortress, abandoned long ago but revisited through correspondence with an old friend.

The artists' story began with a birthday gift from his less than ordinary great aunt, Violet. She presented him with an unusual painter's easel bench-box filled with smelly brushes, old paints, and odd tiny paper books he discovered in oddly shaped hidden compartments. What did the artist unlock from one of those hidden compartments... that changed his life?

Owner of Sugar Art Bake House, a home baking service, proudly shares her story of how her company's name was inspired from fond escapades in her grandma's kitchen. Becky coined her grandma's house The Bake House as a little child! Now she brings those memories and her stories to life in her own business, using grandma's recipes and techniques--even some of her old- fashioned tools. Becky brings her cookie & cupcake decorating classes to life with grandma fun, exciting stories, pictures and videos of the kids' baking adventures, experiments and even funny flops!

A favorite story of mine happened during a workshop a couple of years ago, in Bloomington, MN, where I met Lisa Kneller. It was a fortuitous meeting that has turned into more success than either of us could have imagined at the time. Lisa had spent many thousands of dollars with hopes of learning how to build a large network marketing business. To that date, she had not seen her aspirations materializing. As we talked, I shared my experiences with a network marketing company during the years I'd owned a couple of retail shops. I related to Lisa that I'd regarded the network marketing product as I did every other product in my shop. And although prohibited by the company to display the product as inventory, I had come up with a successful system to place the product into the hands of most every customer walking through my door, making it a function of the entirety of my shop. I quickly rose to a top position in the company, barely recognizing this fact when it was happening, except that is, for the big check that showed up in my postbox.

Lisa and I took a hard look at how she was offering her product for sale. As a result, we decided to use my approach to transition her site to an entirely new interactive level. Her website tells stories of bringing bliss into your life by way of joy, contentment and anti-aging mastery, and a few retail secrets. I'm so proud of Lisa and the wild success she is now experiencing... what a joy!

Go to www.bringmebliss.com and see for yourself! Although Lisa gives me credit for taking her business to a level she never thought possible, it was in the process of consulting with her that I discovered my retail secrets were highly valuable for MLM distributors. Once more, it's all about the story and we developed her brand. Lisa's roadmap to online success was significantly changed by way of a paradigm shift amid our conversations of e-commerce and my brick & mortar shop experience...and of course our many great Skype conversations had definitely paid off! She's getting huge recognition with her blog and podcasts. The sky is blissfully clear for Lisa Kneller these days!

Of course, we all know the story of the shy, handsome kid from Tupelo, Mississippi, who wrote and recorded a song in a Memphis recording studio for his mom. Even though his music stopped in the mid-1970s, his stories, his music, and his successes still live on.
Are you seeing how memorable and how powerful the impact becomes when emotionally charged stories are told? Are you thinking about the tremendous heights your story could take you to? You should be!! It's

here that the "remembering/soul searching" work you did in Step 2 will begin to make real sense to you, maybe giving you a clearer glimpse of the payoff YOU might expect. What family stories or old papers or drawing from school could you attach a memory of inspiration to and write about? It could be a spark of inspiration you've discovered somewhere along the way on your life's journey at work or play, or even just a distant memory you haven't taken the time to research until now. Whatever your story turns out to be, with a little polishing, it could be just the ticket to drawing big attention. It may grab awareness and keep people coming back for more. By connecting real life stories to your *great identity*, you too could become very successful at delivering extraordinary wedding mementos, reeling in your next client, or sharing the joy of baking and decorating with many enthusiastic information seekers looking to buy into your experience AND what you have to offer!

If you're looking to sell product, you won't just be selling hardware anymore. With your story, your unique identity/brand, and expertise, you'll have transitioned yourself into "The Gadget Guy." You're not just a redundant travel agent anymore, no, not YOU. YOU are "The Secret Traveler".

Let me share with you the exploits of my friend Shelley! For the longest time, her ambition had been to become an online niche entrepreneur, but she just couldn't get her stride going in any of the pensive to sober pursuits she'd embraced. You see, Shelley is a beautiful, outgoing, fun loving, affable woman with a natural sense of humor! She can quite easily turn a room of straight laced, business serious, poker-faces into an audience of rip-roaring doubled over, uncontrolled laughing hyenas in about 3 minutes flat! In other words, she has personality plus with memorable humorous impact. Shelley is not the person to offer "leadership thoughts" on subjects not including laughter. Her authentic core talent incorporates making people laugh. She absolutely cannot help herself from throwing funny observations and insights into her speak. It just comes all too naturally and all too quickly to her lips! With the obvious fact that Shelley is of Japanese descent, it became self-evident that her great identity would shine with video blogging (the stage for her humor), offering Japanese products and opportunity for humorous banter. Shelley is a totally chic woman, with a chic story, sprinkled with her very chic sense of humor!

So, why not *get your ACT together* and find YOUR story? Your unique story will set you apart from all others out there, because it specifically belongs to YOU! No one else can tell the story YOU tell! This will elevate you well above the others vying for attention.

STEP 4

BE THE EXPERT YOU ARE

"Experience and consistency are crucial factors of expertise. It's your zone!"
DeAnna Kennedy

I had never really thought of myself as an expert! But over the years I've pushed the boundaries of my fears to bring about new things. I've learned that fear is never enough to stop me if I'm reaching for something I really want to know about. I've learned to love this in myself. I can very easily create adventures by reaching out to learn something new. I've learned to examine and embrace what I've experienced, to take that wisdom to the limit by pushing on to learn every aspect of where my interests have led me, and are still leading me to this day. Music, art, writing and commerce… I can speak, write, and teach from all four areas as an expert.

I love sharing my lifetime lessons, detailing my experiences as I'm doing here, right now, with you. I've worked every aspect of commerce I could get my hands on, from manufacturing to retail and most everything in between. I've seen the good, the bad and the ugly! My wisdom in these areas qualifies me as an expert--a "thought leader" in commerce, e-commerce, and my creative mastery.

So, you might be saying to yourself, "I'd like to be an expert! How can I do that?"
Well, my answer to you is this: Examine your *authentic core talent*. Learn to blog. Write articles. Write a book. Become a "generator" of thoughts and then a "thought leader". Perhaps you have certification in a specialized area. Your education and/or teaching credentials will qualify you as an expert for your topic of choice. Speak out on your subject or subjects of expertise as a "thought leader" and then offer consultation opportunities as part of your platform.

Millions of seekers use the internet to research and find information every single day. Here's a chance for you to provide valuable information for free to other sites as you establish yourself a "thought leader", you'll likely see increased traffic and higher search engine rankings for your own website, adding to your advantage. Always include a link to your site with each tidbit of information you are offering.

- Give your expert content and opinions away freely, it's truly the gift that will keep on giving and come back to you with results.
- Find a memorable "intro and outro" greeting to use consistently for both text and audio, something your view/listener can attach to. Think of it as writing a song and finding that hook line...make it a hit!
- Create videos to accompany your articles, to entertain and further make your point. Give them a useful splash of fun! It's always good to add humor if you can, and put your personality into it, this isn't the time to be shy. Remember the video will only be seen if you want it to be seen, you're the producer and you can re-record as many times as you want to. Try different places to record, take a walk and bring your viewer/listener with you... have fun with it. Splash around in the river of life!
- Write an e-book on your expertise, this automatically elevates you to "thought leader" in your area of expertise.
- Distribute content through online article directories or social media sites, look for online magazines on which to post comments. I found HouseboatInsider.com and I post articles, fun quips and pictures answering questions to engage with the readership.
- Whenever possible take advantage of pushing your information out in order to pull your target- marketed customers in.
- Liberally use the "send to a friend" link when discovering content/videos you deem valuable and worth sharing, this can be very valuable to drive traffic to your site.

- Actively show your expertise by participating in industry forums and social networking sites where your target markets hang out, be an active "thought generator" and "thought leader" in your industry.
- Whenever possible take advantage of pushing your information out in order to pull your target- marketed customers in.

Below are examples of pushing information out...to pull in your target market, so get creative here, the possibilities are limitless:

- An unusual recipe of the week, featuring organically grown spices

- A preview track from your next album, available for five days only

- When is trash not trash? A series of free articles on composting

- A free trial for a web-based service

- An abbreviated online course that leaves the student hungry for more

- A motivational video quote or paragraph for the day, leveraged back to your website

- A "thought leader" quote of the day authored by you, re-enforcing your expertise

You'll reach new readers, so encourage posting and reposting your content, making sure it's linked back to your website. Search engines love links from relevant sites and will reward you in the rankings.

The challenge as a "thought generator" will be to determine how much time, energy, and effort to expend providing free services, information, and enticements. You'll have to decide where to draw the line between marketing and profitability. At this point it will be time to consider substantiating yourself as a professional "thought leader" and contemplate *selling* your thoughts. Continue gathering your followers and enhancing your platform for maximum value.

Here are five effective steps to take to be perceived as an expert in your field of experience:

Step One: Recognize your talent, value it and own it.

Everyone is or could be an expert at something. Keep in mind, our talents for the most part come easily to us, and we often take our talents for granted, not placing proper value on them. The key is to discover your talent, take some time to reflect upon what you've always felt natural talent for, put value on it, own it and then step into it.

Step Two: Declare It.

Once you've committed to owning your expertise internally, say it out loud:

"I am a writer"

"I am an interior decorator"

"I am a travel expert"

"I am an event planner"

Speaking it out is the first step in ownership. Declare it on your business card and a website. Write a bio and include your expertise title.

Step Three: Share It.

Think of your expertise as your *authentic core talent*, and embrace it for the purpose of sharing with the world. You can express it in as many ways as you can think of: a blog, a podcast, live speaking engagements, an online course, coaching, or consulting.

Have confidence in your skill, and offer it up for the benefit of others.

Step Four: Prove It.

Ultimately, the proof of your expertise is when your listeners, readers or audiences have achieved the results they'd been searching for. Ask for endorsements at this point. These could be in the form of testimonials, customer reviews, or case studies. Third-party validations are extremely persuasive to others, thus making them very valuable.

Step Five: Sell It.

Nothing will establish your credibility more than publishing or producing products that flow from your expertise. This could include books and e-books, newspaper and magazine (e-newspapers/e-magazines) articles, articles for newsletters/ online courses, keynote speeches, and coaching programs. Not only does this establish your credibility, but it can also help fund your growth, so you can reach even larger audiences.

Your effectiveness is directly related to your *perceived expert authority* in your field. It must flow organically from your passion, experience, and competence.

Whenever you see traditional titles like professor, chief architect, VP of operations or anything else authoritative, you can expect the person to be an expert. These days, less formal titles such as ninja or guru can also denote expert.

Some would argue that you can only earn your expert status from traditional educational institutions, but I believe that if you have enough knowledge and/or skill and experience to teach or share with others who are looking to learn… you ARE the expert!

So, is it *that* important to become an expert? Yes, and here's why.

There are a number of advantages to being an expert. Two of these stand out with clear benefits.

The first benefit is that everyone wants to work with or buy from the person who has the reputation, credibility, and knowledge of an expert.

This means there is an increase in demand but limited access to the expert; He or She only has so much time to do their work so face/time value increases. The benefits to the expert are that with more demand, there will be greater opportunities to engage with everyone.

- One on one?

- Small groups?

- Large groups?

- Webinars?

- Hangouts?

The second clear benefit of being an expert is purely economics. Demand goes up but the expert only has 8-10 hours available in his or her work day, meaning the expert can set higher dollar value for time, product, or service. Instead of catering to all and competing on price, the expert can be client selective and demand a higher fee.

So, you're probably thinking… "How can I become an expert in my field of interest/industry?"

There are probably as many ways to become one as there are experts out there. If you want to get started immediately, here are the top three activities you must be doing as an expert:

1. Listening…. this involves picking up information from all corners of your industry. Read blogs, magazines, books, go to seminars and workshops, and diligently research online. When you listen carefully and take in every bit of information you can, you will (by default) be improving your skills and getting closer to becoming the expert you want to be. Information really is power.

2. Communicating…. is all about being out there and talking to the people who matter in your industry. Whether it's an interesting meet up, a networking event or your comment on a blog – it's all interaction with your target audience. When you are engaging with the community, you will observe what problems need solving – allowing you to adjust your offering accordingly.

3. Creating.... is where you produce the vehicle and content to showcase yourself with expert status.

For instance, here are a few options for showcasing your status as expert:

Branded Website

Your website brand gives you a base of operation, a place to direct audiences and information seekers to check out your expertise.
Create an interesting blog about your topic of expertise, include video presentations
Add a blog to your website to draw in more traffic, create video presentations of your skill, and show or display knowledge of your expertise claims.
Search for other blogs with similar interests, contribute interesting posts with the goal of guest blogging.
Create video posts that are fun, interactive and interesting to add excitement to blogs with similar interests and topics.

Publications

If you are really serious about becoming an expert, try your hand at writing a book or an e-book.
Write articles of interest before holidays and around seasonal changes pertaining to your expertise.

Podcasts

Podcasting is a rapidly growing space where hosts and guests discuss topics around a specific niche. If you're not ready to launch one of your own, seeking out podcast guest opportunities is a way you can share your expertise with new audiences of listeners.

To get started, search for podcasts related to your industry and find a few that have a format and Q&A style interesting to you. Then, reach out to the hosts with a friendly email, introducing yourself as a potential guest. Suggest why you think you'd be a good fit for their audience.

Before reaching out, follow the podcast hosts to which you feel you can present something of value. Show that you're truly interested in their content with your interaction. This shows professional courtesy and will more likely create more opportunities.

Produce Video content

Again, much like getting into writing an e-book for yourself, if you are really serious about becoming an expert, try your hand at producing video content to get your message out.

Whatever you choose as your medium, the results of your creative output will lead to further promotion, not only by you, but perhaps by others if your content is highly valuable to the end user. Be mindful of personal branding, blogging, social media and networking to reap the full benefit of those out there who are enjoying a lot of attention and could possibly exert a great deal of influence on your behalf.

Speaking of significant connections, meet one of my very favorites. Allow me to introduce you to "Professional Business Connector" Dave Drimmie, from Scotland. In my opinion, Dave profoundly radiates the art of the connection. Take note of his recommendation on the subject: "Don't only focus on closing the sale or the deal, but position yourself so that when you have the opportunity to help someone, you help them, no matter what you think the outcome might be. 20% of those people will take your help and thank you sincerely, but you'll probably never hear from them again. However, that won't matter in the least, because the other 80% will remember you and how you helped them, cementing solid relationships. You'll not only build a great business this way, but you will build a great life for yourself!" Good counsel and it will serve you well! I am so proud to call Dave my good friend! www.davedrimmie.com

STEP 5

CREATE WINNING COPY

"For true brand success, embrace the essential principles of marketing, brand definition, effective social campaigning and consistent storytelling"
DeAnna Kennedy

So, how do you craft the right words and discover the best images to communicate your brand– your *great identity?* All copy and image should be consistent in its message and congruent with your identity, your story, your website, your online/offline image, and your social media presence.

Learn my proven sales copy sequence to take information seekers through the selling process from the moment they arrive on your virtual doorstep, right on through to the purchase process. Think of copy in terms of verbs: stimulate, describe, tell, establish, include, communicate, offer, provide, create, repeat, and develop.

- Stimulate interest with a compelling headline offer
- Describe in detail the problem, the pain, the need or the desire that your offer addresses
- Tell your story and how it applies to your offer
- Establish your credibility as a solver of this problem
- Include testimonials from people who have had success with your products/service
- Communicate about the product(s) you offer and how they benefit the user
- Offer special prices, options, and services on a planned and regular basis
- Provide a strong guarantee

- Create urgency

- Repeat the opportunity to purchase repeatedly within your offer

- Develop your community, your platform

Remember Hansel and Gretel of fairy tale fame? Hansel's plan was simple: "Let us drop these bread crumbs so that together we can find our way home." It didn't work out entirely well for Hansel and Gretel, but the concept is solid: lead your potential customers down the path from display window to cash register with the bread crumbs - tidbits of tasty information, of copy and of image.

Focus on how your product or service is uniquely able to solve problems and make their lives better. Think like a customer and ask "What's in it for me?" "What am I going to get out of this?"

To write compelling copy, it's extremely important that you learn how to listen to what your niche is requesting of you and revealing to you. Listen with concentrated interest, and your writing will profoundly improve. Listen carefully to the phrases your clients are using. Hear what their needs are, what they're really keen to do, and what they'd love to have. Understand what they're struggling with, what feels like a time waster to them, and what irritates them.

When you truly strive to understand your clients, you'll increase your listening skills and in turn you'll learn how to write very good copy. You'll become more persuasive. You'll sell more with much less effort.

So we've talked about listening and learning, now how about the love? Love the fact that you know every facet, function, and quality of your expertise and business. With this in mind, meet your customer where their needs are.

With an excited sparkle in your eye, you love sharing every fact and feature about your product(s) right down to the tiniest detail, true?

Certainly customers want every bit of this information, don't you think?

You love sharing your expertise, you're unstoppable, and you'll talk about how your product beats the competition and serves your customers' needs above all others. You've always heard that enthusiasm is contagious, and you just *know* your customer will become as excited about your product as you are when he or she hears every detail of how superior your product is, right?

Hmm, let's think about this *love* thing for a minute: Is loving your product and having the knowledge and enthusiasm enough to sell your products and/or services? Or is there a frequently *unused secret weapon* you could implement, to be the absolute stellar expert?

Let me tell you a little story about something that happened to me last summer.

I made the decision to increase my workout program, and biking seemed a really fun way to do that. Is there a better way to exercise than to enjoy the countryside on bike paths and backroads?

So, with determination, I enthusiastically walked through the door of the local bike shop on Main Street and explained to the very in-shape athletic shopkeeper (who I'd known for years through local business associations) that I was looking for a bicycle to ride local bike paths and explore the lake areas for exercise. I proudly shared my desire to increase my fitness, sharing with him that I'd come to the conclusion biking was the way to go for me!

The shopkeeper led me around the store determining that a hybrid would be ideal for me and showed me several popular models. His first example had 24 gears, and cantilever brakes. "Oh, and DeAnna, let me show you even more features on a bike over here. This one," he insisted proudly, "has a Shimano drivetrain and disc brakes!" I began to feel a little hazy and lost with all the feature information he was rattling off...I wasn't sure I knew what a Shimano drivetrain should do for me!

Trying not to look bewildered, I started to think that I didn't know enough to be shopping for a bike. It didn't take long, and I was searching for a polite way to get out the door. I heard him say, "How about if I show you to our sale room? Maybe you're looking for something on sale," he pleaded, trying to connect with whatever it was that would get me on track to buy from him. "This is the perfect model for you, DeAnna. It has an aluminum frame and hydraulic disc brakes, and it's on sale. What do you think?"

Huh? I had no idea what the guy was talking about. I ended up feeling stupid at that point because he'd bombarded me with too much information. As a result, I became reluctant to ask him a question about anything. I'd heard enough to know that I didn't know enough to make a decision! I felt like running out the door and giving up on my "bike riding to fitness plan"! Have you ever felt like this? Well, unfortunately it happens all too often …in "brick & mortar" shops and online.

As long as the sales pitch remains focused on features, superior parts, tires and limited warranty, the customer's mind just might be meandering off to something else -like looking for the exit door!

Dot-coms are predictably chocked full of features, specifications, and technical details. After all, we ARE looking for information when we search online, aren't we? Of course we are! Make sure you set your business apart from the masses! Compose your copy by "gifting" the searcher with the very persuasive "feel good factor" your product will give!

- The "feel good factors" of the product will emphasize making the buyer's life easier, better, and more enjoyable!

- The "feel good factors" of the product will inspire the reaction they *must* buy to get that feeling! They buy into the FEELING the features will give them, not the features themselves.

- Buyers are looking to get that good feeling, so give them what they're looking for. Does your copy give your seekers of information reasons they'll *feel good* by using your product?

- Does your copy speak to how your product will make your customers lives easier, or give them more time, or be safer for themselves and their families?

- Does your copy bring your readers a sense of urgency for more enjoyment, more fun, more security, maybe even more relaxation to their lives?

I'll give you an example of what I'm talking about to clarify *"features vs the feel good"*:

I recently shopped online to buy a new oven. As I researched the various makes and models of ovens, I felt inundated and overwhelmed with the detailed features. Most of the descriptions seemed endless as I tediously ticked down lists of special attributes for each oven. For instance, the preheating system, I found detailed technical and much touted lists of superior electronic components. It was never ending…the volts and the watts. (Yawn)

So, to take the boredom out, and to get to what it was I was actually looking for from a new oven, I invented a little "Why Do I Care?" game to get through the process faster. My game goes like this:

"Mr. Oven, you tout a fast pre-heating feature. It's a fact about you; it explains how you work, but why do I care?"

Mr. Oven's answer: "You should care because quicker pre-heating will get your dinner on the table sooner."

My "feel good factor" take-away? I should care because getting dinner on the table in a shorter period of time, will give me more free time. I should care because standing around waiting for my old oven to pre-heat was a waste of my time. Rarely in my efforts to buy the right oven, did the advertising copy emphasize how the oven would make my life easier, such as getting me out of the kitchen faster.

Secret tip to copy writing? Get to the "feel good factors" your product or service will bring before ticking off the features.

Go ahead and use my "Why Do I Care?" game as you prepare sales copy. Allow your products or services to speak to your seekers of information, and "gift" them with the "good feeling factor".

A few more examples for you.

Lawnmower Product Feature: Our lawnmowers have strong hooded blade covers

"Mr. Lawnmower, you have a strong hooded blade cover? It's a fact about you. Why do I care?"

Mr. Lawnmower's answer: "You care because you have a 12-year-old son who mows the lawn and sometimes becomes distracted."

The "feel good factor"? My 12-year-old son will be protected.

Dust Mop Product Feature: Our dust mops have extended scope reach.

"Mr. Dust Mop, you have extended scope reach. It's a fact about you. Why do I care?"

Mr. Dust Mop's answer: "You won't have to stand on a chair or drag out the ladder to dust the fan."

My "feel good factor": I don't have to worry about falling off a chair or a ladder.

Tip: Browse through product and service websites asking yourself "Why do I care?" and "What is the feel good factor?" This exercise will strengthen your copywriting skills…. fine tuning your ability to write fantastic copy that converts!

Emotional benefits such as safety, saving time, reducing cost, increasing profit, becoming happier, feeling healthier and more relaxed, and being more productive will absolutely resonate with your customers' desires.

Recently, I worked with a company that creates beautiful kitchens. We used the "Why Do I care?" exercise for every single word of copy we wrote.

Why will The Cabinet Co. customers feel they MUST buy?

- To FEEL like a professional when they cook and bake

- To FEEL opulent, affluent and prosperous

- To FEEL they can impress their guests in luxury when entertaining

We thought about how the new kitchen owner would FEEL as they visualized themselves in a beautiful new kitchen, feeling the luxury of the countertops and cabinets and possessing all the latest in cutting edge gadgets, appliances, and convenient storage trends. We listed all of those "*feel goods*" as benefits!

Writing sales copy, using real benefits that transition into emotional payoffs, is essential for customer attraction. If you know what your audience desires, dreams of, and secretly wishes for, then emphasize those very feelings as reasons your product MUST be purchased to experience those feelings. Your sales will dramatically increase.

Always be on the lookout for the emotional Why Do I Care? and then tell the story with all the emotion you can stir in!

With all of this in mind, let's go back to my local bike shop story…

So, the next visit I made to my local bike shop, it was to offer him help. He has now drastically changed his approach. He listens very closely to his customers and sells them a vehicle for their exercise plan, for their sightseeing and joy riding, or for joining a bike club...whether he's face to face with his customer or in written copy!

These brakes are the best, even in the rain they brake well, keeping the rider safe.

This bike has 24 gears, so whether you're going uphill, downhill, or are cycling on a flat surface you'll be able to find the right gear quickly and with ease and not feel clumsy.

The ergonomic saddle remains comfortable even after hours of cycling.

The potential buyer now gets a clear picture of how the bikes will be easier to operate, make the rider look like a professional and be more comfortable than bikes from other shops. The shop owner's pitch and written copy are now far more persuasive. He no longer rattles off features, but emphasizes the feelings the rider will get with the purchase of his bike!

Keeping my bike store story in mind, take note that information *without emotional attachment* will most likely become monotonous and boring even if it is necessary information.

You can see from my story, how easily the human mind wanders when information becomes too predictable. To keep your readers' attention, introduce a problem and show how YOUR product can solve or avoid this problem. The best strategy? Introduce a spicy problem here and there to keep your buyer alert and interested, clinging to every tiny bit of your information. Keep the pace and keep your story moving!

Almost any boring feature can be translated into interesting problems that YOU or YOUR PRODUCT have solutions for:

- These disc brakes won't slip when you ride through water.

- The bike has 24 gears, so you don't have to worry about struggling uphill – just click to the lowest gear and go for it!

- The saddle is comfy, even after cycling 20 or 30 miles, your butt will thank you!

Here are a few tips that might help you to describe features and benefits on your website:

Your seekers of information are busy people, looking to swiftly solve their problems. They might be thinking of what to cook for dinner tonight or who can take the kids to dance and soccer practice this week. You have to grab their attention quickly because their cursor is hovering over the back button, and they can click faster than lightning can strike!

Come up with a key emotional benefit for your headline or subhead when writing copy for your product or service.

Use bullet points to list a series of features and benefits, making it easier to read quickly. Mention the most important points first and avoid technical language your reader won't understand.

Realize that empathy for the problems your seekers of information are experiencing is key, you will need to literally sneak into your audience's mind and solve their problems.
Understand thoroughly what your customer needs to eliminate irritations and problems and present them with empathetic solutions within your copy.

Understand how you can fulfill your audience's basic need. How you can help them avoid trouble, aggravation, and inconvenience? How can you make their life easier, pleasant and hassle free?

When you connect your enthusiastic expertise and know-how to your clients' needs and desires …absolute magic will happen! Your credibility will grow beyond your wildest dreams!

STEP 6

YOUR PLATFORM

"Within the links of connections, strength awaits!"
DeAnna Kennedy

Do you remember sitting with your mother or grandmother at the kitchen table, with a stack of Christmas cards and envelopes, carefully copying each address from an address book? I remember my grandma's book had many more names than my mom's book did. Grandma had two big books in which she kept addresses and phone numbers in. We loved sitting with her in the evening as she wrote little notes in the cards to reach out to family and friends, we'd fight over whose turn it was to use the corner of the sponge to seal the annual holiday greetings and affix the stamps. Those lists of family and friends kept us all connected. My grandma said it was important to do that, so we could be available if someone needed our help.

My dad kept just such an address list of his customers in big fat books so he could convey greetings to his customers to stay connected with them. We all had a hand in addressing and stamping those picture post cards. It became a holiday tradition for our family business. When our customers arrived to do business, they'd always comment on how much we'd grown and how much they enjoyed keeping up with what we were doing. They felt they were included in our family of friends and, as a result, came back year after year to do business with the family they had a connection with.

Your journey through life has offered, and continues to offer you happenings to make connections from friendships and relationships. These associations proffer opportunities that can greatly influence your success. Think of the sum of all these individuals as your "platform". Everyone standing on your "platform" potentially contributes support to one degree or another. The more "ready to lend a hand" connections you are engaged with on your platform, the more successful you will be. Make your mind up right now to take a look at your contacts and systematically reconnect, and seriously contemplate how you can offer assistance to them. It is vitally important.

Whatever it takes to gather more connections, do it! It is lifeblood for your victory! Growing your platform is THE single most important task to the fulfillment of your success story!

Here are a few avenues to get started-if you are not already doing so:

- Actively listen for opportunities to offer your assistance to a cause, group or club.

- Intentionally seek out blogs of interest to you and engage with helpful information.

- Reach out with a sincerely written email to those you've lost touch with over the years.

- Actively engage with community businesses, offer to post social media endorsements.

In my opinion, enriching your platform should be something you do every single day. Locate the influencers, the connectors, and the leaders in your life and assist them in achieving their goals wherever you can. Adopt the motto "to give is to gain", a philosophy based on the law of reciprocity. People who adopt this philosophy dedicate themselves to the "giving rather than the get" for themselves. By doing so, others naturally become willing to repay your giving helpfulness by giving to you in return. It's a great way to live life in general and is definitely a standard we can all apply to ourselves!

The people you attract into your life are unquestionably a reflection of you and where you are at, at that moment. In the beginning of my journey I didn't feel like a person of influence, so I set out to emulate a person who was influential. It wasn't until I'd begun acting like an influential person, an influential businessperson, and an influential leader, that I brought about attracting influential people to myself. I used the same methodology with connectors and leaders, and what I found was that giving enhanced my own sense of satisfaction. I became better able to cope with my problems and difficulties, because I got a glimpse of how many people were in more need than I was. Helping gave more meaning to my own life. I found I enjoyed giving the more I gave. I know this for sure: by thinking about how I could help others, I wasn't dwelling on my own problems. The crazy thing is, solutions to my problems and dilemmas have almost always eagerly been offered up when I needed the help.

Basically, you'll need to set this goal for yourself and do what it will take to accomplish it. For example, a goal for yourself might be to add 5 or 10 contacts per day with a system to bring these relationships to life. You might decide 1 or 2 contacts a day is what you have time for. The number isn't as important as the consistency day after day, month after month. Engage diligently and be intentional about keeping your relationships interactive. For example, I create my own form letters making it easy on myself to follow up with acquaintances, thus preserving movement in my direction. I always reiterate a meaningful moment or two from my initial encounter or previous get-together, mirroring a common interest we have and eliciting response/action.

Here's a great thing about on-line activity. The person in front of his or her device can decide whether or not respond or opt-out if not interested in your communications. With that in mind strive to make your messages as relevant and applicable to the framework of *their* interests as you possibly can. Readers will always question whether a message is or is not worth their time, no matter who has sent it. My advice to you is to make your messages warm, personal and meaningful, and direct to your point. Do your best to make group emails sound as though you are speaking to the person doing the reading only.

As you position your business for increased sales, keep in mind that there are many helpful techniques and approaches available to make the most of your email, database collection and platform building. The following is a list of the twenty-four essential fundamental terms for database marketing. Anyone doing marketing today needs to be familiar with as many of these methodologies as possible to maintain and advance growth.

12 Terms You Should Be Familiar with to Get the Most from Your Email List or Customer Database

1) Customer Lifetime Value: A prediction of the net profit attributed to the entire future relationship with a customer. The typical formula is: The average value of a sale, multiplied by the number of usual repeat transactions, multiplied by the average retention time in months or years for a typical customer. Use this calculation to direct your marketing strategy, it will give you an idea of how much repeat business you can expect from a particular customer, which in turn will help you decide how much you're willing to spend to "buy" that customer's attention for your platform.

2) Customer Communication: Personalized customer communication, based on data in a database, along with regular tests, checks and adjustments. It has shown to increase customer retention, loyalty, cross sales, sales, and referrals. Communicating with your customers should be as ongoing as communicating with your friends. This is the #1 principal reason why building your email list/database is so important.

3) Website: The Internet has revolutionized database marketing. A website today, with cookies can be as effective as a live operator, and sometimes more so, directing and enabling contacts to print pictures of the product, print maps, instructions, and many other details. A website is a tremendous standalone base of operation, or in addition to a traditional brick and mortar presence. It's also fantastic for interactive bonding through blogging, essential for successful database marketing today.

4) Email: Despite the vast amount of SPAM, emails have emerged as the most powerful database marketing tool. The ability to contact an audience immediately with new and updating information and announcement details such as "Your product was shipped today and here is the tracking number…" provides invaluable information that continually improves relationships, leading to retention and of course increased contact.

5) Loyalty Programs: A rewards program offered by a company to customers who frequently make purchases. Airlines have been especially successful with their points programs. Interest has spread to grocery stores, hotels/motels, retail stores, coffee shops and a variety of other industries. These retention building programs can greatly increase your database growth through participation.

6) Analytical Campaign Report: Analysis linked to your database to achieve before, during and after campaign reports.

7) Campaign Management: The process of linking directly to online databases for easy planning, selection and coordination of direct mail or email campaigns.

8) Profitability Analysis: A component of resource planning, allowing the forecasting profitability of proposals or existing projects. Profitability analysis can anticipate sales and profit potential specific to aspects of the market such as customer age groups, geographic regions, or product types. We know that some contacts are more profitable than others, however, this has always been difficult to measure. Businesses can now compute the monthly profitability of each customer. Interestingly, many customers are unprofitable. As a result, marketing and pricing strategies can be changed by category to increase profits.

9) Customer Segmentation: the practice of dividing a customer base into groups of individuals that are similar in specific ways relevant to marketing, such as age, gender, interests and spending habits. As your database grows, contacts should be divided into segments usually based on demographics and behavior. Success comes from creating useful segments, and developing marketing strategies for each segment.

10) Multi-channel Marketing: The ability to interact with potential customers on various platforms. In this sense, a channel might be a print ad, a retail location, a website, a promotional event, a products' package, or even word of mouth. Customers buy through multiple channels: retail, catalog, and online. Multi-channel customers buy more than single channel buyers. Using your "customer buying habits" information for personal interaction, when he/she arrives in any of your channels, becomes highly effective.

11) Customer Status Level: All businesses have Gold customers – a small percentage that provides 80% of your revenue and profit. It's important to identify these Gold customers within your database and develop programs designed to retain them. For these customers, you can use resources that you could not afford to spend on all of your customers. Profits come from working to retain your best, and encouraging others to move up to your higher levels.

12) Next Product Analysis: Determining what customers normally buy. From this, you can determine anomalies: customers not buying what other customers are buying from you at the same time. Is it perhaps because they're buying this product somewhere else? This information is used for service providing and customer sales communication.

Growing a large e-mail database and maintaining it is crucial for successful communication and platform building. Here are a few more ways to collect e-mail addresses that have worked for me, I think they might work for you:

- Consider handing out a small print out (not larger than 4"x4") at the next event you attend, with a 'free offer' if they visit your site.
- Be prepared to ask for a business card from everyone you converse with.
- Intentionally create social media posts that friends and family will *want* to 'share'

- Prominently place your contact opportunities on area bulletin boards.
- Collect business card information from bulletin boards (take a picture) and add to your contact list. A posted business card gives permission for interaction.
- Most business networking groups allow visitors to attend free once or twice to get a feel for the group. Take advantage of this opportunity with as many groups as you can find to collect business cards and share your information. Be prepared with engaging information.
- Be on the lookout for every opportunity you have to meet people and get relationships going. Offer free help to your local Chamber of Commerce (ie: distributing Chamber info to local businesses and/or your community). You, of course, will be collecting business cards and beginning relationships.

The importance of your E-mail list:

- Effective e-mails sent regularly build relationships will drive traffic to your website and encourage loyalty with your contacts.
- E-mail allows "event and offer" updates instantaneously.
- E-mail generates immediate response. Providing links within your e-mail to give potential participants the opportunity to interact with you right then and there. You can see the results of your efforts instantly.
- E-mail is targeted. You can easily segment your lists into groups, so your e-mails go to the individuals who are most likely to respond to that particular message.
- E-mail is proactive. Instead of passively waiting for participants to visit your web site, e-mail enables you to aggressively encourage people to engage.
- E-mail expands your reach. Grow your list by sending information to your participants and incentivize them to forward the message onto their own friends and family for a reward.

- E-mail allows you to foster long lasting relationships. Build a regular, ongoing dialogue with those participants who appreciate the routine communication. Those who do not can easily opt-out.
- E-mail will grow your platform. Maintaining and growing your e-mail database will increase the number of people you contact every day, also escalating your sales ratio.

Increasing your email list gives you the opportunity to engage. I've had fun dreaming up games for customers to play for more interaction with them. You might try your hand at something like this if you're so inclined. It can be extremely successful. I've learned that engaging with interactive communication, whether I'm searching for new clients or reaching out to existing customers, is always the winning approach. The application elements of game playing (e.g., point scoring, competition with others, rules of play) as an online marketing technique to encourage engagement with a product or service is highly effective. I've done it many, many times.

The most successful game gave me sales quarters equaling my "4th quarter" sales, the most lucrative months running up to Christmas. The game, I unceremoniously called "The Promotion", permitted me the opportunity to meet every customer who walked through my door. It was a fun way to collect and update customer information and interact personally with new customers while playing an 8-week game, establishing loyalty and familiarity with my shop.

The online and off line versions of this game are available at www.theonlinestorefront.com
Every business is faced with the fundamental question that underlies Platform Thinking: How can I enable others to extend their influence on my behalf for increase beyond my immediate reach?

The answer to that question rests in claiming your achievements and your expertise. Have you authored a book? How many books have you sold? Are you a photographer? Have your photos been published in print or online? Have you appeared on television or radio shows? Have you created podcasts? Have you been a guest on a podcast? Have you hosted events or webinars? Have you appeared as a guest speaker at events? You are entering the sphere of influence of every connection you make. Document with pictures, articles, videos and statistics for all to see. These are your credentials.

People who have encountered what you do and identify with you will eventually connect their followers to you.

An effective platform will extend your influence beyond your immediate reach.

STEP 7

ATTRACT TARGETED SEEKER

"Dress your business for success... as you would dress yourself for success!"

DeAnna Kennedy

It's hard to believe that I worked 14 hours a day, 7 days a week for more than fifteen years! However, brick & mortar almost always requires that level of dedication. Someone has to be present during business operation hours. Over the years I changed the locations of my stores several times, always maneuvering into better location for increased traffic flow. I was always jockeying for visibility and pole position for my targeted buyers' convenience. I located my shops next to high end grocery stores and it worked well. High end grocery shoppers were high end gift and home décor buyers.

Owning a business is a lot of work and requires a lot of space to keep shelves filled with merchandise. Product needs to be moved around and continually kept clean and well merchandised. Labor is extremely costly. My constant presence onsite was required to operate effectively and efficiently. To the contrary, an online storefront, online commerce doesn't require all of the above to function.

The overhead appetite of a brick & mortar store is voracious, the wolf always seemingly barking at the door impatiently waiting to devour money faster than it can be brought in if the proprietor isn't constantly on guard.

Early on, I learned that there was more to turning a profit than creating beautiful surroundings and acquiring the perfect merchandise. The lessons I learned the hard way demonstrated that success depended on the number of people who walked through my front door! I needed to learn how to drive traffic through my door.

Location is crucial, the allure for more traffic flow almost intoxicating it is so critically important, traffic flow IS the absolute lifeblood, vital for every business, online or offline. I became obsessed with dreaming up advertising campaigns to pull more customers through my door day after day after day....

Absolute, unequivocal rule: Traffic flow must meet the business *break-even* dollar amount for survival. Know what your *break-even* is: daily, weekly, monthly, and of course yearly. Note the number of visitors per day, week and month needed for your "ratio of sales" to appear, and don't lose sight of those numbers. Scale the numbers…Work it..work it..work it!!

Today, courtesy of the Internet, customers do not need a map, to get into a car, or to travel miles to walk through the door of a retail establishment to buy what they are looking for. Instead, they can let their fingers do the walking, as they said back in the day. In 1962, when ad agency, Geers Gross, developed that marketing phrase for the Yellow Pages, they had no idea that one day their tagline would have the meaning it does today. Make sure your business is easy to find, easy to remember and easy to get the most from.

The world around us is radically changing, as it always does. We're in the midst of an unprecedented shift of power right now, *favoring the consumer*, fueled by the virtual megaphone at their fingertips through endlessly expanding social media platforms. The old "rule of thumb" (negative word of mouth exchange to 10 people) when a customer was upset, had a bad experience with a product or service, or felt slighted, now seems miniscule. With the "tell all and tell it fast" social media philosophy, negative numbers today can easily jump to 10,000 or more. On the flip side, happy customers now spread their good experiences to thousands, much more than the previous average of three. With those statistics firmly in mind, knowledgeable marketers need to focus on design creativity and initiatives that give the consumer *reason* and *motivation* to share their good experiences. The power shift benefiting consumers can be turned into a commanding advantage by aggressively adapting one of every marketer's favorite presentation conceptual frameworks, the *marketing funnel,* but with a twist.

The twist? Infusing *engagement* into the marketing funnel. With the expansion of the marketer's toolbox to include social media, marketing is no longer about pushing out one way communication. The marketing world is no longer defined solely by impressions; it's now a world of compulsive interactions. Today's marketing must include the customer's voice throughout the process, because whether it's intentional or not, customers will talk online and comment on a brand's marketing campaigns, products, services, and even how a company treats its own employees. It's now not enough to only think about how companies communicate outwardly to customers, it's arguably more important to think about how customers respond and interact to companies directly and how customers take advantage of external reviews thru social media, and with each other. It's extremely important to stay engaged and interactive with your contacts. You do not want to be out of the loop on this one!

Rethinking the traditional marketing funnel: A couple of years ago, Forrester Research published a report on *engagement*, suggesting that the marketing funnel process has become much more complex in today's environment. Although the influencing factors are more complicated, the same simple, visual framework as the traditional marketing funnel can be leveraged for even more effective results. The design needs to account for active engagement during the process rather than looking at it through a lens of inactive messages pushed out.

Here's an example: Traditionally, marketers created awareness by placing carefully planned messages throughout appropriate media outlets. Today, customers can create and spread their own messages about a brand through user-generated content and social networks. Traditionally, marketers would hope to influence seekers of information during the *contemplation* phase through strategic advertising and sales tactics. Today, user-generated ratings and reviews are most often enough to convince a customer to make the purchase. Building loyalty is no longer only about loyalty points programs for repeat engagement. Building loyalty now means entering into a dialogue with seekers of information, encouraging the *exchange of knowledge* and participation in more meaningful ways than stagnant customer feedback surveys or a constant barrage of emails announcing special promotions.

So, while physical location is no longer the absolute for successful transactions, finding opportunities to attract paying consumers to your site is essential. While never ending media opportunities for online retail exists, pay-per-click advertising is probably the fastest and easiest way to get traffic to a brand-new site. Significantly, pay-per-click ads appear on the search pages immediately.

Pay-per-click ads let you test different keywords, headlines, prices and selling approaches. Not only do you get immediate traffic, but you can also use pay-per-click ads to discover your best, highest-converting keywords. At that point you can distribute the keywords throughout your site, in your copy and code, which will significantly boost your rankings in organic search results.

There are many ways for you to attract interest and draw in seekers of information in today's social media climate. The "path of least resistance" for you could be found in positioning yourself on social media platforms where your information is relevant. Join groups where you can exchange your ideas and knowledge of expertise, offering your site for more information and connection.

You must focus on engaging content creation. Good content markets itself. When you put the effort into creating and promoting outstanding pieces of content, the likely result will be more traffic to your website by way of shares and referrals.

Additionally, insert social sharing buttons to your website. Don't just assume that your readers will take the initiative to share your content on their own. Make it easy to add more visitors from social networking sites as well by adding social sharing buttons to your blog posts.

Be sure to answer questions on social networking sites. When you see questions being asked online, provide whatever helpful information you can. Doing this will earn increased website traffic and additional potential customers.

Look to distribute press releases for your achievements. While you shouldn't abuse press release distribution websites to promote insignificant accomplishments, do take every advantage of this traffic stream whenever you have something noteworthy to share.

Capitalize on your website's blog. Publish high-value posts consistently to build relationships with your readers who will be checking back to view your latest posts.

Build a killer email newsletter. Readers who find email newsletters valuable, tend to share them with others. If your current email follow-up sequence is lacking shine, make improvements immediately to increase response.

Publish a fun and informative podcast. A regular, high-quality podcast will increase referred website visitors, and at the same time you'll reach new visitors through podcast directories.
Build a YouTube channel for more visibility. YouTube is a great way to expose new audiences to your brand, leading more traffic your way! This is a fabulous outlet for your creativity to tell your story in your own words (via video) to demonstrate your product and services.

Request that information seekers share your site with others. Ask them to forward your articles or share them on social networking profiles for others who might find them of interest.

Writing guest posts for top industry sites is another very good attention getter. Inquire, to other site owners in your industry, of your interest in penning guest posts for their blogs. Getting your content featured in this way is not only great for your traffic flow – it's also a very good way to build your perceived expertise.

Connect with influencers in your niche. An advantage of getting an authority figure in your industry to share even one of your blog articles could result in tremendous new traffic, subscribers and buyers rushing to your site. Be sure to embrace these key relationship opportunities for personal tutelage as well as for your company's growth. These are the kind of relationships that can bring about amazing developments.

Keep an eye open for and pay attention to up-and-coming social networks. Newer social networks are sprouting up all the time and there could be a significant "early bird" advantage to those who establish a presence on these sites early on.

Check for and eliminate website errors. If search engines aren't able to index your website properly (due to a number of different errors), you might not be receiving all the traffic you should be getting.
Always strive for pillar content. Every website needs to have at least a few pieces of 'mainstay' in-depth, well-written content that will always be of interest to your readers, this will absolutely help drive traffic by way of person-to-person referrals and sharing.

Over-delivering on your company's products or services is a must. From a word-of-mouth standpoint, an over-delivering policy cannot be beaten. When you go above and beyond, customers will not only recommend you to their family and friends – they will positively insist that they check you out. People love expert advice to assist them in decision- making processes, so look for interview opportunities to publish on your site. Expect a big surge of traffic from the expert's existing followers.

Comment on other websites. I can't overstate this enough, leaving valuable comments on other websites' blogs can be a great way to drive traffic back to your own site. Don't miss an opportunity to speak up with good information. Leave the, "Great post!" or, "Thanks for sharing!" comments for others.

STEP 8

TRANSFORM SEEKERS INTO BUYERS

"Welcome! Come join me, sit by my fire, for we all have stories to share!"

DeAnna Kennedy

Inspiring seekers of information to become buyers or engage with your information is like participating in a dance. Sometimes you lead and sometimes you follow, but if the rhythm and the flow stays interesting a relationship will supervene.

When you're building your database, you are creating one of the most valuable business assets you will possess. This applies to brick & mortar businesses as well as online business. Your contacts and seekers of information have given you permission to connect with them. That means:

- They are interested in what you have to offer

- You have the opportunity to develop lifetime relationships with them

- The response is 100 percent measurable

- Engaging funnel marketing, by email is far more cost efficient than print, TV or radio

- Your data base can be sorted and compartmentalized for targeting

Information seekers who visit your site and opt into your database are very hot contacts.

There's no better tool than e-mail for following up with those seekers of information.

Create your interactive e-mail funnel with multiple "click on the buy" buttons.

Every holiday and every seasonal change is an opportunity to reach out to your database.

Keep in mind that information seekers are searching online for solutions and once you have established your expertise, you will be a go to source. The number of "seekers of information" conversions you achieve will directly correspond with your ability to engage and your level of expertise in your chosen field. This is highly scalable. Through your exceedingly important story, checks and adjustments, and your focus on customer solutions, the sky is the limit for you.

Transforming "seekers" into buyers takes a combination of small and large action:

A person, who is just looking, stays passive unless someone nudges him/her to take action, small or large. Think of a ball sitting in the floor: it won't move until it's given a push. And when you do, it starts to roll.

That's what you want to inspire in your "seekers of information". Give them a little bump to get them rolling closer to buying. You make that nudge happen by encouraging them to take a small step, a little call to action inviting them to do something. Ask them to visit your blog, sign up for your newsletter, watch your video or the like. At that point the stage is set for you to eventually invite them to take the action of becoming a customer.

There's an extra bonus that happens when seekers of information subscribe or opt into your space. Their action allows you stay in touch with them, to engage and maintain contact keeping your business at the forefront of their mind for when they're ready to make a purchase. It will be quite easy for you at that time to encourage your seeker of information to take another small step and download a free report or a 30-day trial. What about a money-back guarantee? If you're confident they'll like what you sell, then it's absolutely risk free for both of you.

"Seekers of information" are interested shoppers. Don't overlook "seekers" as just tire-kickers – as in people who look but never buy. It's true that they are not actively engaged in the buying process for the most part, but they are all invariably interested in what you sell in some way, shape or form. Keep in mind that if they weren't interested in your offerings, they wouldn't be looking at your website.

Your "seekers of information" are pausing to gaze at your products or services. They do so for a few reasons:

- They're thinking of buying what you sell, but not right away
- They're gathering more information before making a purchase decision
- They're considering who they'll buy from once they've decided to buy
- They're a fan of yours, and they're admiring what you are offering

Information seekers are fairly engaged with what they're looking for. They rarely happen upon a site just by chance – something led them there, and it's usually their instincts, their interest and their intuition. We like to follow our gut instinct, so keep in mind that semi-idle seekers are always potential buyers. This is where it's very important for them to engage with your site, to get them to take some small action.

Your website will make a first impression, so make it your very best salesperson. After all, it never complains. It doesn't need a pension fund. It won't even ask for a paycheck. It even gives you money just because you gave it a job!

Make sure your website is easy to navigate and easy to buy from. Enable it to engage with your information seekers, to greet them well and nicely encourage them to take that valuable action step. Keep in mind that if your website is not making sales, you'll need to make adjustments.

Have you ever stood in front of a bakery just to take in the delicious bread and cinnamon smells? Tempting wasn't it? Weren't you really wanting to walk through the door and take a bite of something? Picture it in your mind right now. Imagine the morning sun. The noise on the streets. The rows of freshly baked bread, the cakes and pies waiting to be placed in the white boxes to be taken home, and the smiling, proud baker with the tray of pastries...

Now imagine that bakery as an unkempt, less than stellar building with graffiti on the bricks. The woman who held up the tray was missing teeth, had dirty hair and an unappealing greeting. Would you stay in the shop to partake in her bakery goods? Of course not.

Converting "seekers of information" is all about looks, perception, desire, and emotion-- drawing them in to becoming a hot shopper. Your web design is that bakery building, and your web copy is the smiling baker. Make sure both are fabulously good looking, enticing, well maintained, very appealing, and totally inviting. Greet visitors with copy that makes them feel warm and welcome, even if they're just there to browse around. Make a good impression with words that generate positive feelings about your business. They will remember that...and they'll remember you when they're ready to buy.

Here's another tip: Help seekers on your site to find the information they're looking for. Know what their needs are by thoroughly knowing your niche and directing them to what they are looking for as quickly as possible.

Be prepared to answer potential questions before they appear in your information seekers head. Present choices and point out differences along the way. Advise them well. Give them information. Most business owners assume that people know a lot more about the products and services than they actually do. Here's where your expertise will come in handy. Don't forget the "feel good" factor we spoke of earlier. How will your product or service allow your seeker of information to solve his/her problem and feel better doing it?

Help seekers of information remember you!

Treat them well, because they could be your future customers, even if it takes them a year to return and make the purchase. The key is making sure they leave your site with positive feelings and the resolve to come back.

Welcome them, guide them, help them, inform them and let them go with a smile. Stay in touch if possible through your informational newsletter, email funnel and/or blog to show your seekers of information that you take them seriously and you're waiting to be of service to them.

Seekers of information will remember and think favorably of business sites that care about buyers and their best interests and results.

STEP 9

BUILD YOUR BRAND

"Brand definition-the journey of personal and business self-discovery!"
DeAnna Kennedy

My most favorite thing to do when I'm in New York City is to wander about the sidewalks of Greenwich Village, imagining what the old village retail shops must have been like "back in the day". Years ago, most businesses were very small and almost always family owned. The shops were tucked neatly alongside each other in community blocks that served row houses and walk-up flats in growing neighborhoods. Still standing, many original structures housed busy butcher shops, bakeries, and deli shops. These were nestled among mercantile, with the apothecary next door to ethnic restaurants. Laundries, taverns, hat shops, banks, accountants, and law offices lined the streets to serve growing communities. Many still serve in those very places. Overhead signs were proudly hung above the family business buildings, with large display windows revealing what was inside and directing the way in. Many had front entrances with little tinkling bells to signal a customer entering the establishment. These neighborhood shops were the backbone of community life.

New York City's very foundation was built on these inventive, hardworking, entrepreneurial families. I love the charm of this kind of window shopping, looking for reasons to enter and explore new shops, even rediscovering places I'd found on previous trips. This is due, in large part, to effective branding. Successful shop owners have histories and stories, telling their stories in display windows and conversations to differentiate themselves within their community. Just as traditional retailers depended on stories to define and boost their businesses, so too will your unique story and branding efforts play a very important role in the growth and success of your online storefront.

I copied a variety of branding ideas as I carved out my brick & mortar retail years, branding my shops with the various promotions and activities to mark their uniqueness. I learned the power of telling a great story through window treatments, intentionally giving shoppers reason to walk through my front door to see what I offered for sale, just as I had seen and experienced in NYC. My shop became the place to go for neighborhood coffee and comradery, home décor, Godiva Chocolates, beautifully wrapped presents and gift baskets!

Just as brick & mortar retail has a display window, consider the fact that your website home page is the window to display your brand. It's your first opportunity to make a lasting impression on your seekers of information.

As I moved into the online space, I continued to fine-tune my branding skills. My customers loved the decorative window displays in my stores, and I quickly learned to view my website home page as my online display window... ready to entertain and attract attention to draw customers in and keep them on my site. You must keep in mind that shoppers are in a continual state of movement, and if they don't find sufficient reason to stay on your website, with one quick click you're history.

Branding your website will give your customers confidence to keep coming back to you!

As a retailer, one of the most important jobs you'll have is to keep traffic flowing to your business. This applies to online storefronts as well. Your shoppers are looking for reasons to substantiate their time and money, so by all means give it to them. Nothing pulls buyers in and keeps them around longer than a good feeling brought into focus by a window display, a home page telling a story that viewers instantly identify with to ignite emotional feelings. An example would be pictures or phrases inspiring feelings of nostalgia, such as the ones we feel during the holidays (comfort foods, heart & home, love, loyalty, family & friends and patriotism). All of these inspire us "to pause, to look and to stay" to enjoy the good feeling a while longer. This is all a part of effective branding.

I love the good feeling I get walking along, browsing, and peeking into the windows of quaint shops from city sidewalks and doorways to see what kinds of offerings lie within. It's all a part of the experience. As well, I actually clear my schedule for time to grab a chair outdoors on a lovely day to sit at a café table. With my laptop and a cup of coffee, tea or wine in hand, I might browse websites to find interesting blogs and reasons to be drawn in for treasure discovery.

All of this fun stuff that shoppers are inspired to feel through storytelling and branding greatly influenced me when I opened my brick & mortar shop. I say this because it really looked a lot easier from the outside (with all those good feelings) than I discovered it was on the inside. I had professed, "This is gonna be a breeze!" Remember? I was learning the hard way that I didn't know enough to know what I did not know! That gentle breeze mushroomed into a gigantic, uncontrollable hurricane that blew my little raft of a business so far out into the ocean and into unchartered waters, I wasn't sure I could get back to safety. So here's the rest of this story to give you the stark comparison of owning a much less complicated online storefront.

I'd found a great little retail space in a strip mall next to a major grocery store. Location, location, location right? Traffic flow to the grocery store would be fantastic! Easy breezy, or so I thought. I had put in long hours to get my new shop filled with inventory and displayed in a fun, attractive summer beach theme! I suspended beach balls of different colors and sizes from the ceiling. I painted the lower third of the front display windows to look like a sandy ocean beach and the beach balls looked great as my customers looked through the front windows, catching their attention as they approached. I greeted everyone with a Honeydew Melon Smoothie and Hawaiian lei. Memorial Day was upon us…just perfect for getting 'into the spirit' of summer fun browsing and buying!

Then one teeny-tiny problem crept in…a problem I was assured would be taken care of by the building owner when I signed the lease. It turned out there would be no direct access between the strip mall parking lot and the large grocery store parking lot in front of me, so the traffic flow I was counting on from the grocery store would now be diverted into the opposite direction, away from me. The owners of the two properties were feuding with each other...yep, I said feuding! The building owner had told me that the barrier between the two retail centers was scheduled to come down at any moment. Being an optimist at heart, I was sure I could overcome this problem. Certainly I could by appealing to the city if the building owners didn't act quickly enough. After all, the mayor of our fair city wouldn't want the 25 shops that were affected by the barrier to continue to lose business because traffic flow was blocked due to a silly feud, would he? Seemed logical to me that he would act immediately on our behalf. Surely the city officials would step in and order the barrier down for the good of the community. Certainly the mayor would step in for the businesses in his community, right?

WRONG!! I was learning that fighting City Hall was not for the faint of heart and it took a lot of energy, time that would have been better spent concentrating on my business. Nothing was working in my favor, and I was starting to feel the breezes blowing up...a storm was brewing.

I upped my game with more signage and even more welcoming displays at the inconvenient entrance and in my windows to encouraging customers to happily drive around the back of the building piled high with tires. I was desperately trying to distract customers from the hardship of driving around the block to enter. As the days and weeks turned to months I discovered how utterly powerless I was without strong store branding power to pull people in.

However, I fought the good fight and adorned large planters with gorgeous flowers, placed them in front of my shop, added inviting outdoor tables and chairs and strategically placed in front of the window display showing the fun summer products offered for sale.

Those displays drew customers in and a customer base did develop, despite the parking lot barrier problem. I dared to hope the storms were blowing over and my job would be getting easier.

But it seemed the building owner had other ideas. He decided to overhaul the entire heating and cooling systems for his building, only to find out the wiring needed major upgrading. Hmmm the storm was picking up again! The air conditioning was down, and the summer days were HOT. Customers were not going to shop in a 95-degree environment. The summer months dragged on, my costs skyrocketed, and still no air conditioning installation. I struggled to pay for my inventory, and to add insult to injury, a letter arrived from the building owner informing me that I would be required to pay an assessed fee as my pro-rata share of the common area maintenance that included the H-VAC system and barrier removal. All right, any lessons here?

Lesson #1 I learned they were right after all, it's not a good idea to fight City Hall

Lesson #2 Brick & mortar business is risky and not easy to control

Lesson #3 An Online Storefront is much more cost effective and always under the owner's control!

As that steamy summer moved along, I needed to act fast, or I would be going down for the count. I found an electronics company to sublease the space from me. Whew! The first thing I did was put everything on super sale … and created a fun Hot Summer Sale, and with the air conditioning now operable after months, the sale was very successful.

However, in the meantime, I signed another lease in a better location and started over!

The new shop was new construction and located in a much busier and accessible area. I once again invited the community in…. and earnestly continued to build my brand!

By this time, websites and email presented powerful ways to reach out beyond four walls and get the message out. I treated my website home page with the identical importance I'd placed on my brick and mortar display windows. I set out to make certain the branded products displayed on my website looked just as fun and exciting as they did in my windows to entice both e-customers and walk in customers.

I'm hoping you're seeing how vitally important it is to brand your e-business and your products with every opportunity available to you. Spend some time window-shopping on the internet in the type of business you're considering. Gaze into the various home pages of successful websites to see what pulls you in, and take those ideas and implement them for your business.

- What do you see?
- What catches your eye?
- Does the website "signage" engage your senses?
- How easy is it to walk into the website door and find what you're looking for?
- How easy is it to browse around your site?
- How easy is it to purchase from your site?

An online storefront has many similarities to a traditional business. Be committed to budget an appropriate amount of startup money for your website. *Remember* this is your base of operation. Keep in mind that traditional businesses (even right in your own neighborhood) spend thousands of dollars a month on their base of operation, just for the key to the front door. My monthly lease payment per shop was $7,500 and in addition the expenses listed below more than doubled the monthly "nut" depending on the season.

- Utilities
- Insurances, taxes
- Merchandise
- Phones/internet
- Curb appeal treatment
- Employees
- Point of Sale equipment
- Overhead signage maintenance
- Marketing & Advertising

The good news is that the overhead costs for an online storefront (www.theonlinestorefront.com) are significantly lower.

Instead of brick & mortar real estate, your real estate is your website on the Internet.

Instead of location, location, location your traffic flow will come from your data base, marketing and advertising.

Information below is a comparison between traditional brick and mortar vs online storefronts:

- Business mortgage/lease cost (monthly) vs website costs (one time)
- Business utilities (4-5 times more expensive than residential) vs residential cable   fees/website hosting, residential gas and electricity
- Multiple insurance costs vs single plan
- Commercial furnishings vs residential home office set up, (no commercial requirements)
- Merchandise   inventory   investment   vs   drop ship/consignment/turnkey systems
- Brick and mortar storefront set up vs Website home page. (Your unique website "look" and story can be changed out easily with new pictures and information reflecting advertising campaigns and seasons.)
- Employees vs fulfillment services and online customer support
- Location licensing, and State and Federal ID vs State and Federal licensing

Earlier, I shared a story about Lisa Kneller (www.bringmebliss.com) and how I helped Lisa view her network marketing product as a part of her overall retail offerings. Here's the rest of the back story. It might give distributors of network marketing products food for thought.

I had almost reached 10 years in retail, and at this point was the debt holder of two shops. Like many others, I found myself signing up for a network marketing company, mostly because I couldn't say "No" to the person who presented it to me. My shops were busy, so my thought was to set up my MLM product as I would any other product. As most know, distributors are not allowed to offer the product, on a shelf. As a retailer, this made no sense to me whatsoever, but rules are rules!

So, I stepped back and figured out a way to display the product in such a way that every customer entering my shop would be exposed to it, but it didn't stand out as a network marketing product, blending in as just another offering in my shop. The creative presentation for the product along with the daily traffic flow through my shop quickly drove my recruiting numbers through the roof! I was one of the top earners in less than 6 months. It all came down to the presentation of the product and the traffic flow!

So, in reworking Lisa's website, we used the same principles I'd used in my brick and mortar shops to integrate her network marketing product into her brand!

Quick Tips:

- Catch your customer's attention in 5 seconds or less with great photos
- Use simple, contrasting displays for your photo shoots
- Enhance photos with audio and video
- Change your photos often, always ahead of seasonal changes and holidays
- Use seasonal and holiday props for your photo shoots
- Use only crystal clear photos of your product

In conclusion, branding is the essence of one's very own unique story. It's as true for personal branding as it is for business branding. The key is to reach down and pull out the authentic, unique "you". If not, your brand will just be a facade. The power of a strong logo in brand identity is that a simple and clear visual will instantaneously communicate what your brand is about. Very successful brands are able to do this by symbol only (of course that's the Holy Grail of branding) representing the very essence of effective interaction. I believe branding is the identity of a product or service. It's the name, the logo, and the design all at the same time. A brand needs to deliver a clear message, and provide credibility, to connect with customers emotionally. It motivates the buyer and of course creates imperative loyalty.

Logos are vitally important as well, another key component of what creates a strong brand. A memorable logo should support the broader brand strategy. It must also support an even bigger brand stor

STEP 10

BUILD CUSTOMER LOYALTY

"A loyal customer, doesn't just return and simply recommend you,
but insists that their friend do business with you."

DeAnna Kennedy

As I strolled through a flea market recently, I overheard someone ask, "Do you have the Princess Diana Beanie Baby?" I had to giggle to myself. It sure brought back memories of those frenzied days and the over- the- top kerfuffle surrounding Beanie Babies! I'd had the largest one-day retail sales day ever because of the Beanie Baby phenomenon!

It's noteworthy how a $5 retail product, with the added prospect of high resale value as a branded collectible, could become as extremely seductive as it did. It seemed that a low priced item had the capability of being leveraged into big money by the average person, just by collecting little plush toys. Millions of people bought into this illusion, to the tune of 6 billion dollars.

The frenzy for the product was like nothing I had ever experienced. UPS drivers had to lock their vehicle doors even during deliveries to keep anxious Beanie Baby collectors out of their trucks. TY, the manufacturer, even omitted their logo from the shipper boxes so that collectors wouldn't recognize the shipping containers. Long lines would form well before shops opened for business. All of this because of the astonishing demand for Beanie Babies and their perceived value!

Parents had the impression that the return on their investment would be enough to put their children through college. This concept was actually perpetuated and fueled by the collectors themselves, a feeding frenzy so to speak, making Beanie Babies extremely desirable and sought after. The Ty Company merely presented the low cost product as a collectable with limited availability, a birthday, a cute name, a bit of a story and the frenzy blasted into stratospheric success! The take away here is that the customer loyalty plan took on a life of its own with this product.

The power of "customer loyalty" prevailed with this product for many years, making it one of the most successful products of all time. The boost in business for small retailers was a God-send because of the windfall of business. It has been said that E-Bay emerged as a direct result of the Beanie Baby secondary market.

Do you remember Pokémon cards or how about WWF (now WWE) wrestling figures or Precious Moment figurines? Hummel figurines? All collectables are a fantastic method of building customer loyalty through collectability. Call it brand allegiance or customer loyalty, finding ways to "rope in" your customers and keep them coming back is a smart addition to any business plan.

You are exposed to customer loyalty programs daily, not overtly enticing your allegiance to their brand building effort, but imperceptibly encouraging your loyalty through rewarding your purchases. Walgreens now gives you points for every purchase; the customer gets cash rewards. Kohl's offers their "Kohl's cash" ($10 back for every $50 spent). Many businesses offer punch cards, promising a free product for a predetermined number of purchases. These programs work and keep us coming back for more extras, freebees, points, and cash! It works every time!

One of the most important online strategies is to develop every customer's lifetime value. At least thirty-six percent of people who have purchased from you once will buy from you again if you give them reason to come back for a reward. Getting that first sale is by far the most difficult part, not to mention the most expensive. Loyalty programs encourage repeat business and familiarity with your product line or service, offering a healthy offset to acquiring the customer in the first place. Reward your customers for their loyalty and they'll remain loyal to your business.

The Internet offers so many opportunities to reach around the globe for business. It's said that one year of an online business equals about five years in the traditional world of business. Keeping your customers loyal to your brand and rewarding them for their loyalty will be a definite reward for your business. How business is done and where buyers buy has evolved tremendously courtesy of the internet, however, the principles of how to start and grow a successful business has not changed whether online or offline.

If you're thinking about an online business, have just started one or have been online awhile, do a quick review and see if there's a step you've neglected, or haven't gotten around to doing. You can't go wrong with these basics.

ARE YOU READY?

I'M HERE TO HELP YOU

I was nine years old, kneeling on top a lofty, self-described castle-like sand perch, intently spying on my dad and my uncle as they shoveled dusty gray powder from large bags into a huge, white growling tumbler. Next, they began to splash clear water from a green garden hose into the churning, rolling, and incredibly noisy drum. I was mesmerized as the heavy, messy porridge was poured (more fittingly heaved) into two massive holes in the ground. It was noisy and dirty and I was totally enthralled with whatever was happening even though I didn't really know what that was. I just knew I wanted to touch it, feel it and make something with it.

Instead of ignoring my curiosity, my father and uncle carried a shiny aluminum bucket to where I sat perched atop my sand pile, quite easily four to five times as tall as I was. The pail was gloriously filled to the brim with juicy, wet cement. I was instructed to "stay put and keep myself occupied!" I can close my eyes and take myself back to that wonderful day.

Long after the cement hardened between the bricks, becoming our family business, that same sand pile remained a treasure trove for me. I crawled around exploring and discovering every inch of the grainy stuff in search of adornments for my creations. I collected shiny, sparkling stones and rocks, jewel-like pebbles waiting to be polished and put into place. On top of my sand pile workshop, I fashioned cement birdbaths, plant containers and dishes to my heart's content. I just could not imagine a better place on this earth to be and I also knew what I wanted to be when I grew up – anything that allowed me to do something like this forever!

The two seemingly bottomless holes that my dad and uncle sweated so determinedly to fill up gave birth to our beautiful family home and Texaco gas station, bait, and tackle shop. My dad and my uncle had amazingly carved this out of a couple acres of heavily wooded land at the head of a huge lake, appropriately called Sand Lake. A blacktopped two-lane highway ushered a steady stream of curious tourists (trekking up north from Chicago) past and eventually into our family business. Their dreams were cemented into place by sheer determination and perseverance, leaving me with invaluable lessons that have stayed with me my entire life. I don't think that my parents ever called themselves entrepreneurs. They were simply raising a family and building a life where they wanted to be. In doing so, they provided me with a powerful example of leadership and teamwork, lessons that I still use every day to bring the joy of entrepreneurship to others.

Interestingly, the word entrepreneur originally comes from two Latin words. "Entre" means "to swim out", and "prendes" means "to grasp, to understand, or to capture". You may be wanting to grasp or capture something more for yourself but feel as though you'd be swimming too far out with the unknowns of advertising, email lists, inventory, and the like.
Don't stress out just yet.

My intention is to help you figure out what you need to know, to grasp what you were born to do, to capture your unique identity, and to tell your story – in other words to ignite the brilliant flame within you.

I am positioned to come alongside you and show you how to strike the match to help you kindle your *authentic core talent* into a viable online business. I can put you into the driver's seat and hand you the keys to a "done-for-you" site that will get results. You just do the driving.

Here's my website: www.theonlinestorefront.com

I'd also like you to meet my business partner Carlos Morales. I honestly do not know of anyone who understands technology and marketing to a greater degree. He has a proven track-record and a deep-rooted passion for helping small businesses and entrepreneurs.

Carlos and I know that a website has the power to change your business forever, but we also understand that to get results, action needs to be taken. The truth is, small business owners and entrepreneurs usually do not have the time or the internal resources needed to implement the knowledge with which they're empowered.

Below are a few of the discovery processes we will take you through:

- How to take the first steps to a full-time online business
- How to access a complete "done for you" website business
- How to sell across multiple marketplaces
- Access to Drop-Ship and Wholesale Suppliers from my personal list of vendors
- How to maximize profits
- How to source your own product (inventory) from wholesalers
- Acquire necessary business re-sale certificate and licenses to sell professionally
- How to manage your customers for increased customer satisfaction
- How to fund your new business venture (multiple methods explained)
- How to Get Your ACT Together! Aka: your *Authentic Core Talent*
- How to become an expert in ANY product or service category
- How to receive One-on-One tutoring from me personally
- What you need to do to quit your day job and begin earning a full-time income from your online business…and much, much more.

Who will benefit from the www.theonlinestorefront.com proven system?

- Entrepreneurs hungry for the proven roadmap to reliable, increased income from home
- Beginning sellers searching for the proven online retail based business system
- Existing sellers looking for proven fresh new strategy and tactics

- Anyone searching for the proven system for a part-time, online home based business

Here is a simple and brief overview of my teaching modules and what you can expect from them:

1. How to Get Your ACT (authentic core talent) Together and become an Influencer - In this module, I will show you how to discover your expertise, become a recognized leader in your field to establish a powerful brand, attract more customers and grow your platform.

2. The Three Box Puzzle - In this module, I'll disclose the three-piece business puzzle necessary to have in place for financial success. Without all three pieces of the puzzle in place, business failure is certain.

3. Naming Your Business, Logo Creation, Website URL - In this module I cover the importance of choosing a brand name for your business and the significance of developing a stellar logo for your brand.

4. Where do I Find Wholesaler inventory? What sourcing method is best for me? - In this module, I will cover the pros and cons of traditional wholesale buying, drop-shipping and retail systems for acquiring inventory. I'll cover proven activities for long lasting, solid relationships, and why these tactics are significant to propelling your business forward financially.

5. How to Profitably Price Your Inventory - In this module, I'll disclose my proven formula for profitably pricing your product.

6. The Traffic Audubon: In this module, I'll share effective traffic strategies to build and increase your email list and direct the right traffic to the right offers.

7. Your Blog - In this module, I will discuss the importance of writing a blog about your industry and business to elevate yourself to expert status. Blogging is an important part of your SEO (Search Engine Optimization) strategy -- ultimately leading to more traffic.

8. How to Obtain a Resale Certificate an IRS Tax ID Number or EIN for Your Business - These are the numbers you will need in order to identify your business to other companies/wholesalers/drop-shippers so that you can do business with them.

9. Interacting with Your Customers, Gamification, and Quiz Effectiveness - I will discuss how to turn ordinary interactions into powerful calls to action.

10. Social Media & its Importance to Your Business - In this module, we'll discuss how to use social media effectively to drive quality traffic to your online store or website and increase revenue.

11. Facebook - In this module, 1 cover using Facebook to generate more sales for your business, as well as how you can create more awareness for your website and your online identity in general through the use of a professional business page. I will show you how to create effective Facebook ads targeted to your audience.

12. One-on-One Personal Consultations with Me - In this module, I'll share with you what my one-on-one coaching is all about. I'll tell you how you can reach me. I have been selling professionally since 1995. My retail business have given me the hands on education most will never experience. I've learned to incorporate other business models within my brick & mortar shops, even becoming one of the few MLM newbies skyrocketing to four figures a month in less than six months. Today, I work with e-commerce, online and offline businesses, bringing about super-successes through my proven system and consultative processes.

I'm still making music, singing, songwriting and recording. (I've never gotten away from it.) I've embraced it and used it! I've appreciated the value of my talent and have applied it to many other aspects of my life by writing, creating artwork and producing photography just to name a few. I now greedily rely on my *path of least resistance* to get me where I need to go lickity-split! This leaves me with boundless energy to sustain my enthusiasm and to fuel my continual creativity. Why should anyone take the long and difficult energy zapping road, when the personal *path of least resistance* is so very available?

Apply what you have learned in this book. Take action. Turn Your Talent and Experience Into Cash!

Go to www.theonlinestorefront.com to learn more about additional strategies you can implement now to **Find Your Talent Within You and Sell It!**

www.ingramcontent.com/pod-product-compliance
Lightning Source LLC
Chambersburg PA
CBHW060635210326
41520CB00010B/1618